LIFE
LESSONS

HOW I'VE LEARNED TO
EMBRACE **GRATITUDE**, **POSITIVITY**,
RESILIENCE, AND **JOY**

BOB VIOLINO

VBC BOOKS

To my family, friends, and all others who have had an impact on my life and helped me to understand how remarkable it is to be alive.

CONTENTS

INTRODUCTION

Life is always teaching us new things. We never stop learning. Most of us probably associate "learning" with what we did in school, or perhaps some skills we gained through training programs at work or by taking an adult education class at the local library.

While those formal ways of learning are vital, some of the most valuable lessons we will ever learn come from our life experiences. These can be monumental events such as getting married, having children, buying a house, or changing jobs. Or they can be simpler, ordinary occurrences such as shopping for groceries or watching a movie.

No matter how we go about doing it, we are always learning. Life has taught me—and continues to teach me—many valuable lessons, and I feel compelled to share these lessons because they might be helpful to others. Many, if not most of them, have followed challenges such as serious health issues.

In fact, some of the best lessons I have learned have come from dealing with adversities, a few of them life threatening. These include being diagnosed with kidney disease when I was eighteen, surviving a serious automobile accident, and experiencing a sudden cardiac arrest that left me clinically dead for nearly ten minutes. Yes, I've had my share of angels to help me out of the most dire difficulties, and being given these multiple chances to overcome adversity has enabled me to learn new lessons or reinforce old ones.

The challenges we face in life can teach us about new ways to cope, and new ways to appreciate what we have. They can help create better versions of ourselves. The lessons we learn from the challenges we face can also provide us with the strength we need, when we need it. I like this quote that's widely attributed to Walt Disney: "All the adversity I've had in my life, all my troubles and obstacles, have strengthened me... You may not realize it when it happens, but a kick in the teeth may be the best thing in the world for you."

But the challenges are only part of the story. I've also had my share of good fortune. Some of the lessons depicted in the following chapters did not originate from adversities or privileges, but from everyday, ordinary experiences.

Why write this book, and why write it now? After the cardiac arrest and a later episode of heart failure, I got to thinking more about how I should spend my remaining time. What could I do, in some small way, to help others deal with life's difficulties and uncertainties?

I started a blog, *Embracing Gratitude and Positivity*, to share stories from my life. Several people have commented over the years that I should write a book about my experiences, and so it seemed to make sense to write a book that borrows many of the ideas from the blog, but with more depth and context. Each chapter covers a lesson I've learned at some point in my life.

We all have multiple purposes in this life; we're all here for a reason. And I believe that one of mine is to write this inspirational memoir. I'm not a celebrity, professional athlete, or other public figure. I don't have a "platform" to help me reach a lot of people. What I do have is my very own life experiences and knowledge to share. I hope you will gain something from the following chapters.

I must admit, there were times during the writing process when I questioned whether I was qualified to write a book like this. Who am I to provide advice to others? What credentials do I have? I've been a business and technology writer for much of my career. I live with my wife in a suburban community on Long Island, where we raised our two sons.

I've lived what many would consider to be an ordinary life, but I've had some extraordinary experiences that help bring me back to the same conclusion: I am exactly the person to write this book. Ultimately, it's about my life and how I've learned from my experiences—even if I don't always adhere to the lessons I've learned.

As a professional business journalist, I've written many hundreds of articles over the years, but always about other people, and nearly always within the context of unemotional corporate dealings or cold technological facts and figures. There's never any real pain chronicled in those stories, and no one ever cries. But also, there's never any real joy, and no one ever laughs.

As you read through these pages, I hope you are able to glean some insights that help you face your own challenges as well as live a more joyous, purposeful life.

We all are given a limited time on this journey. It would serve us well to embrace the moments we have, no matter what we are doing.

And remember, learning is a lifetime gift!

1

GRATITUDE: THE GIFT THAT KEEPS ON GIVING

Even as young children—before we know how to read, write, or tie our shoes—we are capable of grasping the meaning and importance of being thankful. Research shows that children can begin to understand and express gratitude as early as the age of two, when prompted by others. They gain a deeper understanding of the concept of being grateful between the ages of three and five, when they can begin showing appreciation on their own. Gratitude, quite simply, is part of who we are.

"Throughout history and around the world, religious leaders and philosophers have extolled the virtue of gratitude," notes a May 2018 white paper prepared for the John Templeton Foundation by the Greater Good Science Center at the University of California, Berkely. The center studies the psychology, sociology, and neuroscience of wellbeing. "Some have even described gratitude as 'social glue' that fortifies relationships—between friends, family, and romantic partners—and serves as the backbone of human society," the Center says.

If anyone has a right to be grateful, it's me. I've survived a serious car accident, kidney failure, a life-threatening blood ailment, a sudden cardiac arrest, and heart and respiratory failure following surgery. You might wonder, why would anyone be grateful for these things? Well, in each of these events I was saved by someone or a group of individuals who just happened to be there to help, or who made an extraordinary sacrifice on my behalf.

I've been blessed with more love and support than I can comprehend. Just about every morning I wake up feeling grateful for another day. As the world-renowned poet Maya Angelou said, "This is a wonderful day. I have never seen this one before."

When I decided to start writing a personal blog in the summer of 2023, after many years of putting it off, it was not too difficult to settle on gratitude as a key theme for the posts. The decision to begin a personal blog came shortly after I'd returned home following a five-week hospital stay, and about a year after I had suffered the cardiac arrest. Sometime after that a surgical procedure resulted in heart and respiratory failures that had me on the brink of death. I was grateful for the additional chances at life I'd received, and I wanted to put my thoughts out there for the world to see.

My goal in writing the journal of my experiences and insights was simple. I wanted to help remind readers that all of us have a lot of things for which to be grateful, even when challenges sometimes keep us from appreciating what life has to offer. Despite all the negative things that can happen, whether it's getting the wrong order from Starbucks or having a heart attack, we can find reasons to embrace gratitude as a way of life.

When we practice gratitude, we can enjoy a number of health benefits. These include improved sleep, reduced symptoms of physical pain, decreased blood pressure, reduced stress and anxiety, less fatigue, lower risk of depression, and general wellbeing. In a December 2022 post for the Mayo Clinic Health System titled, "Can expressing gratitude improve your mental, physical health?," nurse practitioner Amanda Logan addresses this by saying, "Simply stated, gratitude should be practiced daily—just as you'd take that magic pill if it existed. Try starting your day by thinking of someone you're grateful for as soon as you wake up. It could be appreciating a friend who sends you funny texts, a teacher who recognizes your child's gifts, or the barista who hands you your coffee and shares friendly conversation. Later, thank that person with a text, note or kind word."

On the flipside, a lack of gratitude can lead to dissatisfaction, resentment, self-absorption, and a negative outlook on life. When we fail to appreciate what we have in our lives, we can experience discontent and feel resentful. We can end up focusing on the negative aspects of life and make bad choices.

A lack of gratitude can also make it difficult for us to form and maintain positive relationships with others, because of all the negative emotions that come from it and the failure to appreciate things. Think about it. Would you want to hang out with someone who whines about what they don't have instead of rejoicing in what they do have?

You can express gratitude in many ways. One is to just say how thankful you are. This might sound obvious, but I think we sometimes get so distracted that we forget to express thanks to people. Vocalizing your gratitude sincerely is a powerful way to convey how you feel. I am fluent in only one language, but I know how to say "thank you" in seven. That's probably because those words are so meaningful that, when I learned them, they stuck with me.

You can take it a step further and express how much the person you're thanking means to you. This is something many of us probably don't do nearly enough. How much the people in your life mean to you—your spouse, partner, children, parents, siblings, friends—is in many cases implicit. But it's nice to actually say it out loud once in a while.

Who knows, you might make someone's day by sharing a kind word. Maybe you can even recite a list of all the things you are thankful for. You have multiple options for reaching out to people, including in-person engagements, phone, or video chats.

Another way to express gratitude is to write a thank-you note. Before email and texting became prominent means of communication in the digital age, people wrote to each other by sending letters through the mail. For the younger generations, this probably sounds archaic and time-consuming. And I have to admit, I almost never write longhand notes or letters anymore, in part because my handwriting is not what it used to be! Still, many people enjoy receiving handwritten letters or cards. It shows that we made an effort to express our feelings of gratitude.

Just recently, my ninety-seven-year-old mother referenced handwritten letters she had received from my dad when they were dating in the early 1950s. She lived in Montreal, and he lived in New York, and this is how they communicated. She still cherishes these handwritten letters.

When you're trying to express gratitude, it's not essential that you pay back someone for a good deed or a kind word. But sometimes a good way to show appreciation for someone is to return the favor in some way. If someone takes care of your pets while you're away, you can return the favor by giving that person a gift you picked up during your travels. Another way to show appreciation is to pay a favor forward: perform a good deed for someone else in response to a kindness you've received.

Feeling grateful can help us to better deal with the challenges we are facing—no matter how overwhelming they might seem. Indeed, sometimes we find ways to be grateful under unlikely circumstances.

I learned this in the spring of 2023, during the five-week hospital stay I mention earlier. My left foot had been giving me trouble for months, and by March 2023 it was swollen, painful and cold to the touch. Multiple cuts and bruises on my toes were not healing. My foot was so sensitive to the touch that even bed sheets brought on discomfort, so I would try to sleep without covers.

A vascular surgeon recommended that I undergo a test called an angiogram to find out what was causing the trouble and presumably to fix the problem at the same time. I was optimistic, expecting the procedure to go off without a hitch and planning for a hospital stay of one night, two at the most. My confidence was reinforced on the morning of the test when the surgeon's assistant ensured me the procedure would most likely go well and that I had nothing to worry about.

That's not how it turned out. The test showed that I had no circulation in my left foot and part of my lower leg. The only way the surgeon could fix the problem was to amputate my foot and part of my lower leg. When I received the news in the recovery room, I was devastated. I didn't want to speak to anyone or hear from anyone. When we had discussed the possible outcomes of the procedure, no one had mentioned the real possibility of amputation. It was a shock.

Walking was a big part of my life. At my peak I was walking between seven and eight miles a day, going well beyond my original goal of 10,000 steps a day. My wife Reneé and I regularly walked in our neighborhood. Sometimes we walked multiple times a day, finding new routes to take to keep things interesting. I couldn't process the idea of not being able to do one of my favorite things.

Reneé, who had heard from the surgeon after the test was completed, helped me to calm down when she got to the recovery room. She explained to me that the surgeon wanted very much to save my foot, but there was no way he could do this. He also said there had been great progress in the development of the prosthetic devices that enable people to walk, despite the loss of a limb.

I was desperately seeking something positive to grab hold of, and this news gave me a reason to be hopeful. In addition, I was beginning to acknowledge the truth that keeping my foot could threaten my life given the condition it was in and the possibility of infections. Because of this, the doctors wanted to perform the surgery in a matter of days, so this scuttled my plans for a short stay at the hospital. And as it turned out, the surgery was scheduled for March 21, which happens to be my birthday.

The night before the surgery Reneé stayed with me in the hospital because she knew I would appreciate her being there. Sometime in the middle of the night I woke up in a panic and said I wasn't sure I wanted to go ahead with the surgery. What if it was the wrong decision to have my foot amputated? Shouldn't I get another opinion first?

Reneé empathized with me, saying she understood how difficult and scary this all must be. She then asked me to think about what my options were. After giving it some consideration, I once again came to the realization that this was the best option. And that realization gave me peace of mind. I was able to go into the procedure with a better, more positive attitude.

What was there to be grateful for in all this? A lot, as it turns out. I got to spend meaningful time with my son Andrew and his then girlfriend, and now wife Nikki, and my son Tim and his girlfriend, Victoria. They all live out of town, so getting to see them was a treat. Reneé had been planning a birthday weekend for months that included a surprise visit from the four of them. They happened to arrive while I was awaiting surgery.

On the Sunday before the surgery, we had a birthday celebration in the lounge that was next door to my room in the hospital, complete with an ice cream cake and gifts. Despite the pain in my foot and having to deal with the fact that I would soon be losing it, I was grateful for the time spent with family. I was also grateful for Reneé planning the original birthday surprise, for my sons and their girlfriends being with us, and for what they all did to arrange this special and unique gathering.

On my birthday—the day of the surgery—I heard from all kinds of family members, including many I hadn't been in touch with for years. They were all sending their prayers and best wishes. It was touching, and I teared up a few times as text messages continued to come in with positive vibes.

The healthcare staff joined in. You know how, when you go to a doctor's office, you're asked to confirm your date of birth? Well, in the hospital it happens constantly. So in the days before my birthday, on my birthday, and even for weeks following, I received birthday wishes from nurses, aids, technicians, doctors, and other healthcare workers. This was in addition to all the things they did to help me get through this difficult time.

Getting birthday wishes might not seem like a big deal. But when you are going through a major health issue and a life-changing event, such good wishes can mean a lot and make a dark situation a little bit brighter. This turned out to be a birthday filled with many unexpected and wonderful gifts for which I'm extremely grateful. And although the surgery was life-changing, it took away all the discomfort I had been experiencing for months, which was also a gift. Time spent with my family was a most precious gift. This was the gift of love, which is priceless.

Sometimes, being grateful can be difficult. It takes a lot of practice and persistence. In the days immediately following the surgery, I clung to thoughts of gratitude. These thoughts kept me from despairing, and filled me with the hope I desperately needed. Embracing gratitude as a way of life, I discovered, is not a "one-and-done" proposition. Our sense of gratitude can be fleeting. And we can be fickle with our attitudes and emotions, depending on what's going on in our lives at a particular time.

One of the biggest distractions and hindrances to gratitude is envy—feeling resentful because of something someone else has or does and wanting the same thing. Envy can overtake us pretty much anytime, even when we don't expect it. When this happens, it can immediately wipe out thoughts of gratitude. Imagine you receive a fantastic gift for your birthday and immediately feel grateful. Then, soon after getting this gift, you glance out the window and see the neighbor's shiny new car, one you couldn't possibly afford but nevertheless want.

All of a sudden, your gift doesn't seem like such a big deal, and maybe you don't feel as grateful. The thing is, there is always going to be someone who has more than you do, and feeling satisfied and grateful for what you have is not always easy. Not surprisingly, a common source of envy is money. A survey of more than 2,000 U.S. adults conducted by the Harris Poll and published by survey sponsor NerdWallet showed that nearly three out of five Americans have felt envious of someone else's financial situation.

But money is by no means the only thing that can lead to feelings of envy. We can be envious of someone else's home, car, appearance, job, family, health, travel, friendships, personality, and so on. Think of how easy it is to feel a bit envious when someone includes vacation photos from exotic places with their social media posts. Or when a friend who recently started a new job gets a great promotion while you're seemingly stuck in the same position.

There are many reasons for us to be envious, all of them unhealthy and in direct opposition to gratitude.

Envy isn't the only thing that can get in the way of gratitude, however. Daily aggravations can easily push us in the wrong direction and even sour our moods for a while. You might be running late for an appointment and, on the way, miss a traffic light because the driver in front of you was texting too long. Or you could find yourself on hold for a call for a long time and then get hung up on and have to start all over again. Maybe your boss is in a bad mood, or you have an argument with a coworker, or a friend, or your spouse.

All of these things might seem minor, but if you are facing more serious struggles such as unemployment or an illness, they can suddenly seem like big deals that make it difficult to be grateful.

One way to bring gratitude to mind when you are feeling envious or aggravated is to immediately think of something for which you are grateful. I try to do this, but I admit it's not always easy. The key is to make it a habit.

As author Joshua Becker points out on his website, Becoming Minimalist, "We would all fare better if we learned to treat gratitude as a discipline of the heart, one that requires attention and consistent practice. Gratitude requires practice when it's easy and even more practice when it's difficult." But, Becker also notes, "Unfortunately, gratitude can be finicky. There are seasons of life where gratitude is easy, when your home is warm, when you're eating a delicious meal, when your child's report card is impressive, when everything is lining up exactly as you had envisioned." At other times, when there is struggle and hardship and disappointment, gratitude can remain elusive. "And yet those are the days we need it the most," Becker says. Those are the seasons of life when strength, optimism and perspective help carry us through.

To help practice gratitude every day, Becker suggests scheduling five-minute periods of thoughtful thankfulness each day, intentionally finding gratitude in the simple joys of life, keeping a gratitude journal, and beginning prayer with a period of thankfulness. All good ideas. I received a gratitude journal book for Christmas a few years ago and I try to remember to use it. When I do, it helps me embrace gratitude even more. It's a satisfying feeling.

We can know gratitude is such a great virtue because it feels so good when others are thankful for something we have done. Years ago, Reneé was volunteering for the Meals on Wheels program, delivering hot and cold meals to elderly, sick, or handicapped people in the area who were housebound. At one point, she got very busy with work and was unable to make the deliveries and asked me if I could help.

Being unemployed at the time, I had plenty of free hours so was able to step in. Along with my son Andrew, who was three years old at the time, I went to the nearby church that provided the food to pick up the packages, then drove to the first home on the delivery route.

A frail, elderly woman answered the door and immediately burst into a bright smile when she saw Andrew. He'd gone with Reneé on deliveries, so many of the people on the route had met him. The woman asked us to come into the house and sit down at her kitchen table. She lived alone and I could see she had to struggle to walk even a few feet. We stayed there for just a few minutes, listening to her talk about her life, and the entire time we were there I could see that the woman was thrilled to have us as visitors.

I realized then that delivering the food was only part of the service Reneé provided for these people. The companionship, even for just a few minutes, meant as much to them as the meals. As we left the woman's house to go to the next stop, I felt a sense of warmth, accomplishment, and joy that I hadn't experienced in a long time. We had done something to help someone feel a little better, and her gratefulness became mine.

We can't be grateful all the time, but we would do well to train ourselves to be grateful a great deal of the time. We have to keep at it until it becomes a habit, because gratitude is a gift that keeps on giving.

2

THERE'S POWER IN POSITIVITY

Positivity, the practice of being or tendency to be positive or optimistic in attitude, is one of the hallmarks of a satisfactory existence. There's a great quote attributed to Mahatma Gandhi that sums up the value of positive thinking: "Keep your thoughts positive because your thoughts become your words. Keep your words positive because your words become your behavior. Keep your behavior positive because your behavior becomes your habits. Keep your habits positive because your habits become your values. Keep your values positive because your values become your destiny."

On any given day, we can wake up to a number of negative thoughts and feelings. We might be overwhelmed by problems at work, health issues, family or relationship difficulties, financial hardships, worries about world events, and so on. Unfortunately, we are sometimes stuck in a cycle of negativity that can create a downward spiral that leads to sadness, hopelessness, and depression. Getting to a state of positivity isn't always easy, but it has many rewards.

I was at a gathering recently where someone I knew came up to me and began talking about my blog. First, she noted that she was a regular reader of the blog, which I was glad to hear. Every writer wants people to read their content. But then, to my surprise, she mentioned that the posts were upsetting to her because they were so positive. The stories actually made her feel worse about things.

Needless to say, this wasn't the kind of feedback I was expecting, given that the whole point of the posts was to make people feel better by thinking about things to be grateful for and to feel positive about. But it got me thinking that some people, for whatever reasons, have a difficult time embracing positivity.

There is, however, such a thing as being overly and unrealistically positive; it's called "toxic positivity." As described by *Psychology Today*, toxic positivity is "the act of avoiding, suppressing, or rejecting negative emotions or experiences. This may take the form of denying your own emotions or someone else denying your emotions, insisting on positive thinking instead. Although setting aside difficult emotions is sometimes necessary temporarily, denying negative feelings long term is harmful because it can prevent people from processing their emotions and overcoming their distress."

The publication also notes that there is nothing wrong with showing positivity, optimism, and gratitude, and that those traits help people to flourish. Positivity only becomes problematic when it functions to reject negative emotions, it says.

Life can certainly be difficult, but we need to look for the positives around us to help us get through the challenges we face. It is precisely because life can be challenging that we need to look for things to be positive about. Ultimately, it comes down to the choices we make about which directions to pursue and how to view the world. There are always ways to look for positive elements in life, even during struggles that might seem insurmountable. The power of positivity is undeniable.

Dealing with negativity is part of being human. This is especially true when we are facing a daily flood of discouraging negative information from multiple sources. All you have to do is scan the feed on your computer or mobile device, watch the local news on television, or read the daily newspaper to find story after story about negative events.

An old saying in journalism states, "If it bleeds, it leads." The idea is to attract readers through fear, violence, conflict, etc. Social media sites such as Facebook, Instagram, X, and even LinkedIn can also subject us to a flow of disturbing news or obnoxious opinions.

There is a phenomenon called negativity bias, also known as the negativity effect. It is a learned bias where, even when positive or neutral things of equal intensity happen, the things of a more negative nature such as unpleasant thoughts, emotions, or social interactions, have a greater effect on our psychological state than neutral or positive things. A December 2019 article by psychologist Catherine Moore, posted on PositivePsychology.com, says negativity bias can explain why we often do the following:

- Recall and think about insults more than we do about compliments

- Respond more, emotionally and physically, to unpleasant stimuli

- Dwell on unpleasant or traumatic events more than pleasant ones

- Focus our attention more quickly on negative rather than positive information

"Even when we experience numerous good events in one day, negativity bias can cause us to focus on the sole bad thing that occurred," Moore writes. "It can lead us to ruminate on small things, worry over having made a bad impression, and linger on negative comments."

Stuff happens in our lives, even minor things, that can make us think in negative ways. On several occasions, my computer crashed while I was working on assignments for clients. As a result, I lost some of the content I was writing because I didn't have a chance to save it before the crashes. As any computer user knows, these experiences can be frustrating. Each time, my irritation would last for a short while because I saw the technological failures as a drain on my productivity. In the scheme of things, these were minor setbacks. But they show that even small things can push us away from being positive, if even for brief moments.

I've faced some significant events that have thrust negativity into my life. I have had seven jobs in my career since graduating from college, not counting my time as a freelance writer over the past two decades. Two of those jobs ended in layoffs, and one resulted in my being dismissed, in part because of health issues. Each of these instances provided me with reasons to be negative. In some cases, far more so than others.

One incident years ago involved receiving hemodialysis treatments after going into kidney failure. The nurse in charge of my care did much more than teach me the technical ins and outs of dialysis. She was keenly aware of how important it was for me to accept dialysis as a treatment, and to deal with the emotional struggles that can go with it. She did everything she could to put a positive light on something that can be extremely traumatic.

One night when I was in the clinic, the husband of a woman

who was also undergoing these treatments stopped by my room to chat. I'd seen him before while I was receiving a treatment, and he seemed like a decent guy.

"I can't see how you can go through this," he said after we had exchanged small talk for a brief time. "I wouldn't do it." I was surprised at his comment. "What do you mean?" I asked. "You would just let yourself die?" He said that he probably would and I began to get indignant. "What about your wife?" I asked. "If she had the same attitude, she'd be dead. Is that what you'd want?" He didn't answer. "You must not think much of your own life," I finally said.

Before the next treatment, I mentioned my encounter with this man to the nurse. Later on, when she was standing by the door talking to me, she noticed the man in the hall. "You can't hang around here," she said, in a not-so-pleasant tone. "Please stay in the waiting area and don't come in here again." She then shut the door in his face.

Dialysis is not easy. There are many challenging aspects of it. But one of the keys to success is to have a positive attitude. This can make all the difference in terms of seeing improved health. My nurse was keenly aware of this, and that's why she banished the man from the area where I was receiving treatments. It might have come across to the man as rudeness, but she was making the point that negativity was not welcome in the treatment room.

After that incident, I started to focus on the benefits of hemodialysis more than I had before. I knew the treatments were keeping me alive, and that filled me with a sense of wonder. It was humbling to think that, were it not for dialysis, I wouldn't be alive. When I looked at the treatments as giving me a new chance at life, they took on a much more positive meaning. I began to convince myself that I was fortunate to have the opportunity.

It really is about taking an upbeat approach to life, about choosing to be positive. We need constant reminders of this. I have a book by Norman Vincent Peale, *Positive Thinking Every Day*, that has a brief suggestion for each day of the year. Here are a few that I find helpful:

> "Every day remind yourself of your own ability, of your good mind and affirm that you can make something good out of your life."

> "Give thanks daily for your blessings. Get the habit of thinking happy thoughts. Go out of your way to make other people happy. There is your formula for real happiness and enthusiasm."

> "How you think about a problem is more important than the problem itself—so always think positively."

I try to remember these words as I go about my days. Sometimes it's easier than others to focus on them. Positive thinking and optimism can lead to a number of health benefits, according to the Mayo Clinic. These include:

- Increased life span
- Lower rates of depression
- Lower levels of distress and pain
- Greater resistance to illnesses
- Better psychological and physical wellbeing
- Better cardiovascular health and reduced risk of death from cardiovascular disease and stroke

- Reduced risk of death from cancer

- Reduced risk of death from respiratory conditions

- Reduced risk of death from infections

- Better coping skills during hardships and times of stress

Those are some convincing benefits! Given all this, it's a wonder anyone would not want to take the time to develop a more positive outlook on life. There are four simple ways to do this, according to a September 2019 article in *Psychology Today* by Tchiki Davis, Ph.D., a consultant, writer, and expert on wellbeing technology.

One is to use and strengthen the positive pathways in your brain by spending more time thinking about positive things. For example, memorizing and recalling lists of positive words. Another is to look for the silver linings. People with a positive attitude always find the upside of things. If you want to change your perspective, practice finding the good in situations. Anytime you are down about something that has happened to you, look for at least one benefit.

The third way is to practice random acts of kindness. This is something we all should do more, including making efforts to be kinder to those around us. It could be paying compliments on how someone looks, offering congratulations for some achievement, milestone, or event, or bringing food to someone who is ill. Finally, the fourth way is to smile, laugh, and generally try to enjoy life. Deciding to enjoy yourself more is a key step in developing a positive attitude. We can choose to be upset, angry, anxious, fearful—or not to be.

A couple of things I would add to this list are, one, surround yourself with as many positive people as possible, because positivity can rub off. And two, watch uplifting or motivational videos online.

The Mayo Clinic suggests we stop negative self-talk to reduce stress. "The positive thinking that usually comes with optimism is a key part of effective stress management," it says. "And effective stress management is associated with many health benefits. If you tend to be pessimistic, don't despair—you can learn positive thinking skills." Positive thinking doesn't mean ignoring life's less pleasant situations, the clinic states. "Positive thinking just means that you approach unpleasantness in a more positive and productive way. You think the best is going to happen, not the worst."

Positive thinking often begins with self-talk, the clinic goes on to say. "Self-talk is the endless stream of unspoken thoughts that run through your head. These automatic thoughts can be positive or negative. Some of your self-talk comes from logic and reason. Other self-talk may arise from misconceptions that you create because of lack of information or expectations due to preconceived ideas of what may happen." If the thoughts that run through your head are mostly negative, the clinic says, your outlook on life is more likely pessimistic. On the other hand, if your thoughts are mostly positive, then you are likely an optimist who practices positive thinking.

Psychologist Catherine Moore recommends a few practices to overcome the negativity bias. One is achieving self-awareness and challenging negative self-talk. "By checking in with yourself throughout the day, you can start to recognize any thoughts that are running through your mind—both helpful and unhelpful ones," she writes. You can also look at your own behaviors to get a better understanding of what's serving you and what isn't, she notes, and from there, you can start to tackle these head-on, challenging them and replacing them with more useful ones.

Another tip she suggests is to practice mindfulness to become more attuned to your own emotions. Through guided meditations, reflection, and other mindfulness techniques (such as breathing exercises), you can begin observing your feelings and thoughts more objectively. Finally, savor the positive moments. "When you stop and take some time to drink in a positive experience, you're savoring it and creating memories for the future," Moore writes. "Building up your store of positive mental images and feelings can help you address the imbalance that negativity bias predisposes us to."

I try to do this when I travel to someplace new or revisit a favorite vacation spot, or attend an event like a concert or a ballgame. By letting myself truly focus on the good feelings I'm experiencing at the moment, I get more positive bang for the buck. The fact is, I don't even have to leave home to enjoy positive experiences. Every day has the potential to present positive moments to savor.

Many of the public and private comments I receive from my blog posts have been about how people are trying to overcome cycles of negativity in their lives. Some of them are truly heartbreaking. Struggle is part of the human condition, but we must not let it overwhelm us.

We all need to look for things to be hopeful and optimistic about. We must try to think of the good aspects of a situation that happens to us, rather than wallow in the negative. The positive news is that we can all do this if we try.

3

THERE'S NO TIME LIKE THE PRESENT

Are you putting off getting started on something that has been nagging at you for weeks or months? Well, it might keep nagging at you until you get it done. And when you finally do take action, there's a good chance you will feel at least some level of satisfaction and gratification—if for no other reason than that the constant nagging will have stopped.

Most of us are guilty of procrastinating now and then. We put things off, rationalizing that there's no rush to get started. We make excuses for delaying, perhaps blaming it on the distractions of daily life.

People procrastinate for a variety of reasons. Some of us are concerned that the outcome of our actions might not live up to our expectations. We want perfection the first time out and we let that stop us from even trying. Others are distracted, anxious, or fearful about whatever it is we need to do. Perhaps we want immediate gratification and are not willing to accept long-term payback for finishing something. Or it could be that some tasks just feel too overwhelming—or even too tedious.

Whatever the reason, one thing is clear: the thing we put off doing doesn't get done, and that might set off a chain reaction of negative outcomes. A study of more than 3,500 Swedish university students published in 2023 suggested that procrastination was linked to subsequent mental health problems such as depression, anxiety, and stress; disabling pain in the upper extremities; unhealthy lifestyle behaviors such as poor sleep quality and physical activities; and worse levels of psychosocial health factors including higher loneliness and more economic difficulties.

That's a lot of potentially bad outcomes just from putting things off! The students were followed over a nine-month period, based on self-reported procrastination—which the study defined as voluntarily delaying an intended course of action despite expecting to be worse off because of the delay—and self-reported health outcomes. Other research also has shown that procrastination can be harmful. Whether it's an occasional behavior or a chronic tendency, procrastination is a form of self-regulation failure that's linked to negative outcomes.

What's especially unfortunate about putting off achieving our goals or realizing our dreams is that we are robbing ourselves of the gratitude and sense of accomplishment we can feel when we do things we've been thinking about for a long time. Studies have shown that many people near the end of their life regret not the things they did, but the things they didn't do, such as taking risks and being brave in the face of opportunity.

Doing things now rather than putting them off can lead to some great benefits. One of these is reduced stress. When you delay the completion of a task or the beginning of a new opportunity, the incompletion of the task or the failure to jump at an opportunity can lead to feelings of anxiety and stress. You will feel unfulfilled until you do what you need to do. Conversely, if you take action, the stress, anxiety, guilt, and even general sense of failure will likely vanish, either immediately or in a relatively short time. You will be off and running, finishing the work you started or launching a new adventure that might take you to places you've never been.

Another benefit is an increased sense of accomplishment. You can take something off the to-do list because you will have gotten it done. You can make a mental note about something you accomplished, and obliterate any feelings of regret at not having moved ahead. Overall, you will have a stronger sense of control over your life, as you move toward completing your tasks or grabbing at opportunities more efficiently. You can boost your overall wellbeing and mindset.

You're by no means alone in your battle to get through procrastination. "We all procrastinate important tasks once in a while," notes the article, "Overcoming Procrastination," on the Johns Hopkins University Academic Support website. "The problem arises when we're procrastinating all the time and not recognizing it as a habit. While eliminating procrastination completely is an unrealistic goal, there are several things you can do to limit the number of times or duration of time you procrastinate for."

One is to identify your daily goals. "In order to stop delaying important tasks, you have to identify those tasks in the first place," the article says. "If you start the day by identifying all the things you have to complete within that day, you will hold yourself more accountable compared to when you identify them as you go. Every morning, make a list of goals you want to accomplish on a piece of paper, your notebook, or the notes app and tick them off as you go."

Another tip is to set specific goals. "Identifying your daily goals isn't enough to overcome procrastination; your goals must be specific," the article asserts. "Replace vague goals with measurable ones by setting a duration of time you want to work... Set specific goals in the beginning of your day so when you begin, you know exactly what to do and how long to do it."

A third thing you can do to minimize procrastination is to set realistic goals. "By deciding to do more than you are able to in a day, you inevitably disappoint and demotivate yourself," according to the article. "A big part of overcoming procrastination is setting realistic goals. Instead of beating yourself up about not being able to read a hundred pages in a day and then not reading at all, decide to read fifty pages in a day. Setting realistic goals will keep you motivated to continue ticking things off your list at a speed that is more comfortable and productive for you."

Another good practice is to throw some easy tasks into your day. "Remember to include easy tasks on your daily to-do list," the article notes. "Just because a task is easy doesn't mean it doesn't take up time or that it isn't important. This serves as a reminder that there are tasks that you are completely capable of doing to give you energy for the harder tasks. Whether that easy task is doing laundry, drinking eight glasses of water a day, going for a walk, or calling a friend, make sure you are reminding yourself of the things you are capable of to help you through the things you doubt yourself about."

Finally, try to include accountability. "If you have been having issues with procrastination for a while, starting out your journey to productivity can be challenging," the article notes. "It may feel easy to slip into old habits without realizing. This is why it is important to [create] accountability." Ask your spouse, other family member, or a friend to check up on you at the end of the day, or week, or month to see how you have been doing in terms of overcoming procrastination. While these suggestions are aimed at an academic audience, they can easily apply to anyone in any circumstance.

If you feel called to do something, or an urge to accomplish a task that's been on your to-do list for a while, there is no time like the present to get started. It's one thing if we put off doing a chore like taking out the trash or mowing the lawn until we feel like it. But it's another thing entirely if we delay doing something that has been a dream or a goal of ours for months, years, or even decades.

Are you thinking about starting a company? How about writing a song, or a book of your best poems or short stories? Do you feel that you have a gift such as drawing or painting and want to put it to use? Is there a scientific discovery waiting for you to uncover? Do you have a symphony in mind that you've not yet put down on paper?

Okay, maybe some of these are lofty examples. The point is, you might be just the person to achieve one of them. Imagine if Alexander Fleming never got started on his work that led to the discovery of the antibiotic penicillin, or if Johannes Gutenberg never invented the movable-type printing press that started the printing revolution, or if Leonardo DaVinci wasn't able to push himself to put that first dab of paint on the canvas that would become the *Mona Lisa*. We don't have to compete with these history-changing achievements, but I think we are obligated to follow our own dreams.

I put off starting my own blog, *Embracing Gratitude and Positivity*, for years before I finally got around to launching it in the summer of 2023. It's something I long thought would be fulfilling and take advantage of my writing experience. Still, I just kept putting it off.

Coming up with topics and actually writing the posts can be a lot of work and sometimes frustrating. But the gratitude I've felt from having the opportunity to provide some positivity to people who need it has been well worth the effort.

What really pushed me to start sharing the stories in the posts was the realization that time is finite. Life is short. If not now, then when? In my case, the impetus for beginning the online journal were a few serious health issues that were abrupt reminders of my mortality.

In some ways I felt a sense of urgency to do this. We should not need a major scare or life change to push us into action, though.

Sometimes our decision to follow a pursuit can influence others to do the same. For instance, a reader of my blog wrote me to say one of the posts encouraged her to finally do something she had been thinking about for a long time: retire from her work and spend more time doing things that are truly important to her. This response was especially gratifying to hear. I hope her decision has brought her gratitude and joy.

I've received many other comments from people since starting the blog. A number of times, I've heard from people who wrote that my words were just what they needed to hear at that moment. To me, this provides reinforcement that the blog was a good thing to do.

On occasion, the things we really want to do are not front and center in our minds. That might be because we are overwhelmed by daily concerns and obligations. Maybe if we look for ways to be more efficient with our time, we can start that project that's been calling to us. I've compiled a list of things you might be putting off, or that you might consider doing in the future. Some are relatively mundane, while others are potentially life changing. In either case, I hope you can find something on this list that inspires you to get started on your own exciting journey.

- Start a new business out of your home
- Climb a mountain
- Compose a song
- Make a quilt

- Make a career change

- Get married

- Take up a new hobby

- Learn to swim

- Become a volunteer at a soup kitchen

- Coach a youth sports team

- Start a YouTube channel

- Make a spiritual pilgrimage

- Learn to play a musical instrument

- Try out for a role in a play

- Adopt a pet from an animal shelter

- Build a treehouse in your backyard

- Earn a new or advanced degree

- Run for public office

- Learn a new language

- Buy and ride a bike

- Retire and travel to interesting places

- Start a blog

- Write a book

A new initiative does not have to be a major undertaking. Indeed, it can be something as simple as calling a relative, or an old friend you haven't had contact within a long time, or fixing a leaky faucet. If there is something you really want to do, don't wait. Don't give in to procrastination. As Benjamin Franklin said, "You may delay, but time will not."

Take a chance. Start now. You will be glad you did.

4

THINK THIS WAY

When you think about it, we're almost always thinking. We don't think about the fact that we're thinking, we just do it. We think about family members, friends, work, projects, health, hobbies, plans, news events, the weather, sports, and countless other things. We spend so much time thinking, and it is so engrained in our lives, that, for the most part, we don't think about how we are thinking.

Thinking in and of itself is good. We think about looking both ways before crossing a busy street. But more critical kinds of thinking can actually be good for our brains. Critical thinking is a fundamental skill that enables us to analyze and interpret information objectively and rationally. By evaluating and interpreting information, we can form sound judgments and make informed decisions.

Older adults who regularly take part in word and number puzzles have sharper brains, according to an online study led by the University of Exeter and King's College London, published in the *International Journal of Geriatric Psychiatry* in May 2019. The more regularly adults aged fifty and over did puzzles such as crosswords and Sudoku, the better their brain function, according to research involving more than 19,000 participants. Researchers asked participants to report how frequently they engage in word and number puzzles and to undertake a series of cognitive tests measuring changes in brain function. They discovered that the more regularly participants engaged with puzzles, the better they performed on tasks assessing attention, reasoning, and memory.

There is potentially a downside to how we use our brains, however, which is what some people in the psychology field call "cognitive distortions" or "unhelpful thinking styles." We all experience this kind of thinking from time to time, but it is not healthy, as you can probably guess from the labels. The trick is to catch ourselves when we fall into these patterns and try to get past them, and in the process, create helpful ways of thinking.

Unhelpful thinking styles are "ways that our thoughts can become biased," according to Psychology Tools, an organization that provides resources and guidance to mental health professionals. "As conscious beings, we are always interpreting the world around us, trying to make sense of what is happening. Sometimes our brains take 'shortcuts' and generate results that are not completely accurate." These shortcuts can be bad for us and for anyone we encounter. They can happen suddenly and without any warning. "Cognitive distortions happen automatically—we don't mean to think inaccurately—but unless we learn to notice them, they can have powerful yet invisible effects upon our moods and our lives."

Dr. David Burns, a psychiatrist, adjunct professor emeritus in the Department of Psychiatry and Behavioral Sciences at the Stanford University of Medicine, and author of the book *Feeling Good*, has put forward ten specific styles of unhelpful thinking. I've included them here, along with my suggestions for how to turn them into helpful thinking styles.

ALL-OR-NOTHING THINKING

This is the tendency to evaluate your personal qualities in extreme, black-or-white categories, according to Burns. When we perceive things in terms of all or nothing or black and white, that does not leave us any wiggle room. We look at things, including our qualities and capabilities, in extremes.

So, for example, in my job as a writer if I complete a work assignment for a client and it doesn't turn out perfect, I may think I've failed. Or, if I oversleep and end up missing a meeting, I might assume that the entire day is going to be miserable. It's easy to see why this approach to thinking is not healthy. Evaluating ourselves or others based on extremes is not realistic, because life doesn't typically work that way.

This kind of thinking can keep us from trying things for fear that we won't do them perfectly. If we give ourselves some leeway and replace the blacks and whites with grays, we can take away the fear. So, rather than chiding myself for turning in an imperfect assignment, I can acknowledge that I did a good job and work to make the needed corrections. Instead of concluding that a day will be miserable because of a rough start, I can shake off the early disappointments and make the most of the rest of the day.

OVERGENERALIZATION

This is when we draw broad conclusions about our abilities, performance, or even our worth based on a single incident. And it's so easy to do. After you fail a test, you might assume that you are always a failure. Or, if you are ejected following a job interview, you may conclude that you will never find a job. Maybe your boss gives a thumbs down on a proposal you submitted, and you decide this is going to happen every time you submit a proposal, so you stop trying.

This kind of overgeneralization might distort your thinking because you reach conclusions that are too broad, given the circumstances. I find it helps when I try to bring context and perspective to particular events, rather than generalizing too much. If we keep open minds about things, we're less likely to fall into this way of thinking.

MENTAL FILTER

Try to imagine that you have achieved something impressive. Maybe it's running a successful event for your company, preparing a big meal for your family on a holiday, or teaching a class and seeing many of your students win academic honors. You get great feedback from a lot of people who rave about your skills and what you've accomplished. Then there's that one person who says something negative about the event, or the meal, or the class. Rather than soak in the positive feedback and adulation, you focus on—even obsess about—the one criticism. This is thinking with a mental filter, and it can really do a number on us.

Years ago, I headed up a special issue of a magazine I was working for at the time. It was an enormous amount of work, the largest issue in the history of the magazine, and I was pleased with the results. Lots of other people were as well, and were very complementary. Then, one editor pointed out that there was a minor error on one page—out of more than 250 pages of content.

Needless to say, this was irritating and I found myself focused on it—but fortunately, for only a brief period of time. I quickly reminded myself that some people feel a need to point out flaws in others' work, and in many cases, we just have to ignore it and focus on the positive. This can be difficult, but with practice and a bit of tweaking of the mental filter, we can do it.

DISQUALIFYING THE POSITIVE

Related to mental filter is disqualifying the positive, which is when we dismiss or downplay positive events, experiences, achievements, or feedback. We essentially think these positive elements of our lives do not count, they are flukes, and as a result, we retain a negative perception of ourselves—even though all the evidence points to the contrary. We transform positive experiences into negative ones by finding reasons to discard them.

In a 2013 article, "Ten Types of Cognitive Distortions," Burns describes the ability to transform neutral or positive experiences into negative ones as a "spectacular mental illusion," and one of the most destructive forms of thinking. "An everyday example of this would be the way most of us have been conditioned to respond to compliments," he writes. "When someone praises your appearance or your work, you might automatically tell yourself, 'They're just being nice.' With one swift blow you mentally disqualify their compliments."

How can you counter this? Embrace the positive! When you experience positive events, achievements, or feedback, remember that they do count.

JUMPING TO CONCLUSIONS

Have you ever made a determination about something without having all of the facts? I know I have. We do this because, in a lot of cases, we come to conclusions based on our previous experiences or what appear to be obvious facts.

If your favorite baseball team is ahead by ten runs in the bottom of the ninth inning, you can reasonably conclude that it's likely to win. But if someone you know doesn't return a smile when you meet and you decide they must be upset with you, or if someone you don't know doesn't return a smile and you conclude that they are being rude and think little of you, these are unwarranted, negative conclusions.

There have been occasions when I've emailed someone multiple times and gotten no response, and concluded that the person was ignoring me, only to find out that they had been in the hospital because of a sudden illness. Variations of this kind of thinking are mind reading, when we think we know the intentions or thoughts of someone; and fortune telling, when we have inflexible expectations of how things will turn out before they even happen.

It's easy to see how jumping to conclusions could have a disruptive impact on relationships, jobs, even our own emotional wellbeing. The trick is to not always make assumptions based on appearances. Think it through before coming to any conclusions.

MAGNIFICATION AND MINIMIZATION

Magnification is what happens when we look at our errors, fears, or imperfections and exaggerate their importance. I can relate to this. There have been times when work was going slow, and an assignment I was going to receive from a client fell through. I'd think to myself, "That's it, my freelance writing career is probably over." I'd see a negative pattern based on a single occurrence. Other times, when I've received a reward for an article and thought little of the honor, I'm minimizing, which is when we look at our strengths or accomplishments and downplay them.

"I like to think of it as the 'binocular trick' because you are either blowing things up out of proportion or shrinking them," Burns writes. "You're looking at your faults through the end of binoculars that makes them appear gigantic and grotesque… When you think about your strengths, you may do the opposite—look through the wrong end of the binoculars so that things look small and unimportant."

This sounds like an easy fix: put away the binoculars and observe things as they really are.

EMOTIONAL REASONING

Emotional reasoning is when you take your emotions as evidence of the truth, according to Burns. "Your logic, 'I feel like a dud, therefore I am a dud'," he writes. "This kind of reasoning is misleading because your feelings reflect your thoughts and beliefs. If they are distorted—as is quite often the case—your emotions will have no validity." We are often guided by our emotions more than logical thinking, so it's important to not let them affect how we think about ourselves and make decisions.

Emotional reasoning plays a role in nearly all cases of depression, according to Burns. "Because things feel so negative to you, you assume they truly are," he writes. "It doesn't occur to you to challenge the validity of the perceptions that create your feelings." To counter this, try not to let your emotions have an effect on how you perform at something. Feelings come and go. Facts are facts.

"SHOULD" STATEMENTS

Sometimes we try to motivate ourselves by saying, "I should do this" or "I must do that," Burns says. "These statements cause you to feel pressured and resentful," he notes. "When you direct should statements toward others, you will usually feel frustrated… Should statements generate a lot of unnecessary emotional turmoil in your daily life."

When the reality of our own behavior falls short of our standards, our shoulds and shouldn'ts create self-loathing, shame, and guilt, Burns says. We're all human, and our actions and those of other people will inevitably fall short of expectations from time to time.

An editor once pointed out to me that I was using the word "should" frequently in an article advising organizations about how to better implement a cybersecurity strategy, and that this might come across as condescending to some readers. He suggested I use different wording. But as I recall, he didn't say I *should* do that! It was good advice, and I've been avoiding that word ever since.

LABELING AND MISLABELING

This is when we place unjustified labels on ourselves and others. We might do this because we're frustrated, angry, depressed, discouraged, or for some other reason. Regardless of why we do it, it's not a helpful way to think.

Some time ago, a guy parked his car in the street, partially blocking our driveway, as he chatted with the neighbor who lives next door. As time went by and he wasn't moving his car, I thought to myself, "This guy must be an idiot," placing that label on him. But then I reminded myself that I didn't know anything about this person other than that he was parked in front of our house and apparently knows our neighbor. For all I knew, he devoted much of his free time to volunteering at a soup kitchen, or was going through emotional issues.

Regardless, it was a relatively minor annoyance, and using a negative label was neither fair nor productive. We can also do this to ourselves sometimes when we mess up, which is also unfair and unproductive. So the next time you think of saying, "Oh, I'm such an idiot," don't!

PERSONALIZATION

This type of thinking is "the mother of guilt," Burns writes. It's when you assume responsibility for a negative event when there is no basis for doing so. "You arbitrarily conclude that what happened was your fault or reflects your inadequacy, even when you were not responsible for it," he writes. We can blame ourselves when someone else—our coworker, friend, spouse, child, client, teammate, whoever—has done something wrong. We assume, for some reason, it's our responsibility and then feel as if we have failed.

Personalization gives us a sense of responsibility that forces us to carry the burdens of everyone else and, Burns notes, it confuses influence with control over others. We can influence to some degree virtually anyone with whom we interact. But we can't control them. What other people do is ultimately their responsibility, not ours. We do not need to assume responsibility for their actions or inactions.

If you're struggling with any kind of extreme, unhelpful thinking, please consider seeking professional help. It's good to be aware of certain negative ways of thinking. Acknowledging these unhelpful thinking styles can be, well, helpful.

5

CELEBRATE THE MUNDANE

Much of life is not particularly exciting. Many of us have the same routines day after day: we get up, take a shower, get dressed, eat breakfast, brush our teeth, go to work, complete tasks, have lunch, attend meetings, do some more work, go home, cook and eat dinner, watch television, read, go to sleep. We also perform the same chores on a regular basis, like making the bed, cleaning the house, doing the laundry, taking out the trash, shopping for food, doing paperwork, completing homework, washing the car, feeding the pets, mowing the lawn, watering the plants, etc.

Pretty blah, right? Wrong! All of the things we do in life, all of the mundane tasks—even those that seem to be the most boring—are things we can celebrate. And by celebrate, I don't mean putting on a party hat and breaking out the champagne. I mean it more as acclaiming rather than reveling, taking the time to acknowledge that these things are all part of life and therefore are a gift to be cherished.

It is so easy to take the day-to-day events of life for granted. Much of the time, you probably don't even give a lot of thought to—much less appreciate—what you are doing. But it's these small, simple moments that likely make up the majority of your waking hours. The ordinary things in life, in most cases, are not the spectacular, and therefore they do not inspire us to feel gratitude or much else. How many people get excited about something like filling the car with gas or cleaning the bathrooms?

Not surprisingly, even the term "mundane" can have a negative connotation. Similar words in a thesaurus are not exactly electrifying: humdrum, dull, boring, tedious, monotonous, repetitive. Many people use the expression, "same old, same old" when asked how they are doing, indicating that things are the same as usual, and implying a sense of monotony and tedium. But when we turn the ordinary, day-to-day routine on its head, we can find ourselves appreciating the daily tasks and chores in ways we never anticipated.

Some time ago, I had to go to the hospital for a sudden medical issue. I was there for five days, which actually was a considerably shorter stay than previous hospital visits I've had. But this time I got to thinking about the need to appreciate the "ordinary" time we have at home, at work, at the grocery store, and how it can be more valuable than we realize.

While I was in the hospital, I was living in a different place, sleeping in a different bed, eating different—and not always edible—food. There was a lot of noise at night, sometimes the lights were too bright, there was unfamiliarity. During one particularly long stretch of time, I was prohibited from eating or drinking anything prior to having a procedure done. It's not that the hospital is such a dreadful place to be. As one of the nurses pointed out to a disgruntled patient who was none too pleased to be there, we should be thankful that there are hospitals around for when we need them. But an experience like going to the hospital takes away some of our freedoms, our independence, and our routines. We are decidedly out of our comfort zone, and eager to get back into it.

So this particular hospital stay served as a reminder to me that maybe those ordinary, seemingly drab days are not so bad after all. Every once in a while, we need to stop and feel thankful for the mundane and the simple things in life. We need to treasure those little moments, even if they might not be particularly exciting or memorable.

The ordinary and routine parts of life do not have to be negatives. We can find graces in the familiar things; we just need to look for them. Our day-to-day routines can also serve as a nice contrast to the more exciting things we do in our lives. There are even many potential health benefits to having daily or weekly routines, according to health information website WebMD. These include:

- **Reduced stress level.** When you have a plan for your activities, you will feel like you are more in control of things. You will have made a lot of decisions beforehand.

- **Better sleep.** By keeping a consistent sleep schedule, you will likely end up better rested. Good sleep can provide people with an emotional boost, and, if you have difficulty falling asleep, having a bedtime routine can help.

- **Improved health.** WebMD says meal planning makes it easier to stick to a healthy diet. In addition, you can use a routine to boost your physical activity or to take medications at the right time.

- **More happiness.** If you have a set schedule, you can build in time for enjoyable activities, whether it's reading, playing in a sport, hiking, traveling, birdwatching, or whatever. Such downtime is good for your mental health.

Having routines is especially important in situations such as addiction recovery, bipolar disorder, and other mental health problems, according to WebMD. "People who are recovering from addiction need to replace bad habits. Planning ahead and staying busy can stave off boredom, which could lead to relapse. Good habits can improve self-image and confidence, which are often lacking in people with addiction disorders."

Routines might help with bipolar disorder, according to one study in which people used a tracking device to monitor their schedules, WebMD says. Those with bipolar disorder might have more sensitive body clocks, researchers say. In another study, scientists studied circadian rhythms, which are the periods of rest and activity that you go through in a typical day. "Disruptions of these cycles triggered depression, mood disorders, and other problems," WebMD notes. "The researchers also found that people with disturbed circadian rhythms were more likely to be lonely and less likely to be happy."

It's the simple and the ordinary things in life that we sometimes need to stop and think about. Sometimes it's good to rejoice in the mundane. Those quiet, ordinary activities—getting chores done, finishing a work assignment, reading a book or magazine, browsing the Internet, watching the sunset or sunrise, taking a walk in the neighborhood, doing a puzzle, or just sitting outside and soaking up the sun—can be a blessing that we all too often take for granted.

I wrote a blog post on this topic, and every so often since then I have been trying to think about how lucky I am to be working on a writing assignment in my home office, or sitting in the den watching a show or a movie on Netflix, or brushing my teeth before I go to bed. We are blessed with a finite amount of time in our lives, and a good deal of it will be spent on things we will not remember. But even though they might not stand out, those are moments to be treasured.

6

LOOK FOR JOY

A lot of us use the terms "joy" and "happiness" interchangeably, but there's actually a difference. While happiness is typically more fleeting and tied to external circumstances, joy is a deeper and longer lasting sense of wellbeing and contentment. If I had to pick one over the other, I would choose joy.

Compassion International, in an article entitled, "What Is the Difference Between Happiness and Joy," notes, "Joy can share space with other emotions, such as sadness and fear. But happiness can't. Happiness isn't present in darkness and difficulty. But joy can be. If we choose joy, it can transform our difficult times into blessings and our heartache into gratitude."

Unfortunately, all kinds of things can provide obstacles to finding joy in our lives. These include dwelling on negative thoughts or focusing on the negative aspects of life rather than the positive, having unrealistic expectations, the fear of change, lacking gratitude, comparing ourselves with others, coping with a physical or mental health issue, dealing with regrets about past actions, experiencing too much stress, looking for perfection in an imperfect world, and on and on.

While modern technology has made some tasks easier, stress levels have stayed the same or increased, according to an article on the Mayo Clinic Health Systems website, "Tips for Embracing Joy in Daily Life." About one quarter of U.S. adults have reported they are so stressed most days that they are unable to function, and many experience at least one stress-related symptom, such as headache, fatigue, nervousness, or feeling depressed, according to the article.

"Joy is a powerful emotion and harnessing it can be a remedy for stress-related burnout," Mayo Clinic Health Systems says. "Contentment and joy can positively improve physical and mental health and overall wellbeing." The health care provider distinguishes joy from happiness: "Often, happiness is the emotional reaction to what is happening around you. Whereas joy isn't reactionary and often is driven by internal motivations like working toward a goal or finding a purpose in life." Sources from the Mayo Clinic Health Systems provide a few tips for discovering joy:

- **Focus on what you can control.** Many of the things that stress us out are out of our control. For instance, we can't control the weather, how others treat us, things that are in the past, or natural disasters. To create joy, focus your attention on things you can control.

- **Express gratitude.** Be thankful and express appreciation for the things and people around you. Practicing habits such as keeping a gratitude journal can help us shift our focus to appreciation and blessings rather than problems and challenges.

- **Keep perspective.** Some of the decisions we make or the situations we are in can have serious, long-lasting effects on our life. But oftentimes those things that seem important today might only matter a little or not at all in a few years. As you strive for joy, try to remember to keep in perspective which situations and decisions are important and which are not.

- **Assume good intent.** When we're already feeling stressed, we can view any additional inconvenience or misunderstanding as unfair and an intentional barrier to joy. In most cases, people are doing their best with the information and skills they possess, and their actions are not malicious or spiteful.

- **Concentrate on building relationships.** To varying degrees, we all need social interactions with others. For many people, helping to lift others up creates a sense of purpose and joy. If building healthy relationships is a key part of your life, you can find happiness and joy.

Oftentimes our ability to experience joy is based on our outlook at a particular time. Years ago, I was laid off from my job as a business and technology writer at a publishing company called CMP. It was actually my second go-around at the company—interrupted by a job at another.

When I first started working at the company in the early 1980s, it was a family-owned business that offered lots of opportunities for advancement from within. On my first day of work, the president of the company introduced himself to me in the elevator and welcomed me to the organization. CMP held social events to build morale. One such event is where I met my future wife. In short, it was essentially a dream company, and even though it became much more "corporate" following an acquisition by a larger company, I still assumed I could have a job there for life if I chose to stay.

I was wrong, and some of my earliest reactions to losing my job were disappointment, shock, fear, and anger. How would I find a new job in what was then a struggling economy and a difficult time for the technology writing market? Within a short period, though, I was looking at the situation in an entirely different way. My perspective had changed, and I saw not impending calamity, but a wonderful opportunity to become my own boss and be responsible for my own success. I knew it would likely take hard work, persistence, and patience, but I was determined to make a go of it.

It is now more than two decades since I launched my own freelance writing business, and I have never looked back. Becoming a freelance writer proved to be a great decision. The first step to making that fateful decision was to change my perspective on events.

Perspective is just one of what the Dalai Lama and Archbishop Desmond Tutu call the "Eight Pillars of Joy" in their book, *The Book of Joy: Lasting Happiness in a Changing World*. The book provides many insights about life, but I found the section about the pillars to be particularly valuable. In addition to perspective, they include humility, humor, acceptance, forgiveness, gratitude, compassion, and generosity. It's worth taking a closer look at each of these pillars.

PERSPECTIVE

When you look at things from different points of view, or with a broader perspective, even the most challenging situations can seem at least a bit more tolerable. Your perspective is your outlook on the world at large, and fortunately you have control over this outlook.

Think about that. You can take virtually any situation you face and be the master of how you feel about it. That gives you the option of taking a positive approach to even a negative situation.

HUMILITY

We live in a world that venerates power, fame, and professional and financial success. People practically worship celebrities and professional athletes. And many of those same people often use the word "humble" in the wrong way when they are receiving accolades.

Even ordinary people can become obsessed with getting more social media likes or views. Many of us, either consciously or subconsciously, want to be more powerful, wealthier, better looking, or smarter than we are. It's easy to understand why humility would not be high on the list of attributes people would aspire to in such an existence. To be humble is to be ranked low by others, as in a person of humble origins.

So why would it be included in this list, you may be wondering. The fact is, there is much to like about humility. Humility is not thinking you are better than others, or having a low, down-to-earth view of your own importance. It means being free from pride and arrogance, expressing yourself in a modest way, and having an accurate opinion of yourself.

Think about a time when you found yourself really admiring a person who is being genuinely humble and sincere. Especially someone in a position of power, or who has accomplished great things. I consider someone like Mother Teresa to be a model of humility. Although she was one of the most well-known and admired people in the world, she emphasized the importance of humility and practiced this virtue in her daily life and in her interactions with others, especially those living in poverty.

In my experience, humility often equates to kindness. I've come across hundreds, maybe thousands, of people in my personal life as well as in my four decades as a writer and editor. Those I have been most impressed with and drawn to are the ones who aren't overly impressed with themselves at the expense of others.

I find one of the most effective ways to feel humble is to go outside on a clear night and look up at the stars for a few moments. When I do this, it makes me feel incredibly small in this unfathomably large universe in which we live. It is at such transcendental times that I have also felt a sense of calmness and peace, and that has brought me joy.

HUMOR

It's funny, there are a lot of television shows or movies I have watched and enjoyed over the years, and then had no real interest in viewing again. But I have watched episodes of *The Honeymooners* countless times and I still find myself laughing out loud. The show, and the characters featured in it, bring me joy.

It's true: laughter really can be the best medicine. We can experience both short-term and long-term benefits from laughter, according to the 2023 article, "Stress relief from laughter? It's no joke," by the Mayo Clinic. The short-term benefits include enhancing your intake of oxygen-rich air, which stimulates your heart, lungs and muscles, and increases the endorphins that are released by your brain. Others are stress relief and the increase and then decrease of your heart rate and blood pressure. In addition, laughter can stimulate circulation and aid muscle relaxation, both of which can help reduce some of the physical symptoms of stress.

As for long-term effects, laughter might improve your immune system, relieve pain by causing your body to produce its own natural painkillers, increase your personal satisfaction, make it easier to cope with difficult situations, help you connect with other people, and improve your mood. If you can find a way to laugh about your own situations, you can feel your stress begin to fade away, according to the Mayo Clinic article. This is true even if the laughter feels forced at first.

I specialize in dad jokes. Many of them aren't all that funny, but they still manage to make people—myself included—laugh. One time I received a book of dad jokes from one of my sons as a Christmas gift. I read through the jokes when everyone was gathered around. And even though some of these jokes were truly groan-inducing, the more I read, the more everyone started laughing. It added to the holiday joy.

Having a good sense of humor is a positive trait to have at any time, but it can be especially important when you are facing personal challenges or observing so much negative news going on around the world. When we join others in laughing at something funny, it somehow connects us. The ability to laugh at ourselves and our own limitations is an important part of finding inner peace and joy.

ACCEPTANCE

We have to play the cards we've been dealt in this life, and make the most of what we have in hand. When problems arise, our lack of acceptance can make the difficulty all the worse. And sometimes not accepting things can even put us in greater danger.

When I was in kidney failure many years ago, I refused to acknowledge that I was very sick. I was in denial, and didn't want to continue the hemodialysis treatments my doctors had put me on. One night, I arrived at the hospital for my scheduled 5 p.m. treatment, still stubbornly convinced that I did not need the treatments. At first, I wasn't going to go, but Reneé talked me into it.

I was in a bad mood, not at all looking forward to going, and when I arrived at the dialysis unit at a little after 5 o'clock, a nurse told me they weren't ready for me and that I should go to the waiting area until I was called. "It looks like you're going to have to wait an hour or so for a machine to become available," the nurse said. This was the excuse I was hoping for, and I pounced on it. "Please tell the doctors that I'm going home," I said. "I don't need these treatments and I didn't want to be here in the first place." The nurse said she'd try to reach the doctor on call that night.

I went to a payphone—not many people had mobile phones in those days—and called Reneé to tell her I was coming home. She tried to calm me down and said she was driving up to meet me there. In the meantime, I waited in the hallway for the doctor to arrive. When he did, he told me in no uncertain terms that I needed the treatments. Then he began walking in a bizarre way, back and forth in front of us, shuffling his feet and waddling like a duck at the same time. He's lost his mind, I thought. Here was this distinguished, world-renowned nephrologist looking like he'd had a few too many alcoholic beverages.

"Do you see how I'm walking?" he said. "This is how people walk when they have advanced neuropathy. This is how you'll end up, or worse, if you don't do these treatments."

And just like that, I accepted the fact that the treatments were indeed the best course forward. Dialysis wasn't easy, but it provided me with a lifeline until I was able to get a transplant.

There is a reason the "Serenity Prayer"—"God grant me the serenity to accept the things I cannot change, the courage to change the things I can, and the wisdom to know the difference"—is so popular. It makes a lot of sense. The first part, about accepting the things we can't change, makes difficulties easier to handle. While to some acceptance might seem like a giving up or defeat, it's not that at all.

It is being realistic about the world and our place in it, and trying to make the most of any situation.

FORGIVENESS

Of the eight pillars of joy, this might be the most difficult one to embrace. We all struggle with forgiveness—for a variety of reasons. We might be afraid of being hurt by the same person again, so we reason that forgiveness is pointless. Or maybe the person who caused the pain refuses to acknowledge fault. Perhaps we are so angry that we crave revenge, or maybe we're concerned that forgiving will signal an acceptance of bad behavior.

Sometimes when we have been wronged in some way we just want to stay angry at the person or situation that caused the hurt. We can learn to feel comfortable with anger as the go-to and stay-with emotion when someone has done us wrong. Despite the difficulties, we have all been blessed with the ability to forgive, to let go of the angry feelings and thoughts we have toward someone or some group of people who hurt us. We can replace those feelings with positive ones.

Maybe the most surprising thing about forgiveness is that it is so difficult. When you consider it, forgiving someone does not necessarily help the person who committed the wrong, but the person who was wronged. When we are able to forgive, we make a conscious decision to let go of the resentment and anger we're harboring and replace those feelings with positive thoughts. We put aside our lingering bitterness toward a person who, in many cases, might not even be aware that they've done something to hurt us. If you look at it this way, it's easy to see how forgiveness can lead to feelings of joy! While forgiving someone does not mean absolving them of blame, it does mean deciding to let go of the negative feelings that can actually wind up causing us more harm than the original wrongdoing.

GRATITUDE

This pillar of joy resonates with me especially well because it's something I try to practice every day, and is therefore one of the focal points of my blog. We all have a lot to be grateful for, even if it doesn't feel that way sometimes. Life can throw challenges our way that make it hard to be grateful. Despite all the things that can go wrong, all the big and small challenges we face, we can find reasons to embrace gratitude as a way of life.

I cover gratitude extensively in the first chapter of this book, so won't go too deeply into it here. But it bears repeating that research has shown that practicing gratitude can bring significant benefits for our health, including better sleep, reduced symptoms of physical pain, decreased blood pressure, and other results associated with enhanced health. Being grateful comes in many forms and it can help us to better deal with the challenges we might be facing, no matter how difficult they might seem.

And it's important to distinguish between feeling gratitude and expressing it. When we feel grateful, we enjoy the positive vibes that come from that. When we express gratitude, we pass along that positivity to the person or people for whom we are grateful.

Suffice it to say, gratitude can put us on the fast lane to joy.

COMPASSION

Compassion is responding with care to someone else's distress. It's closely related to empathy. But while empathy refers to sharing in the emotional experience of another person, compassion adds a desire to alleviate the person's distress. I've been blessed to be the recipient of compassion on so many occasions and from so many people as I dealt with various health issues. Nurses and other healthcare professionals who work in hospitals and doctors' offices possess a remarkable amount of compassion.

There are multiple ways to practice compassion. We can truly listen to others when they are speaking to us, especially when they are sharing something important. We can refrain from making judgments about others, accept them for who they are, show them the respect they deserve, speak to them with kindness, or apologize when we have done something wrong. And we can encourage others as they aim to achieve goals or try to overcome challenges.

Those are all things that are typically easy to do! Having compassion for others—and ourselves as well—can help make a positive impact on our own lives. Just think about how good you feel when you help someone who is struggling in some way. How can you not feel joy when you are giving or receiving compassion?

Compassion leads to joy by creating a positive cycle in which the act of caring for other people or alleviating suffering fosters a sense of connection and purpose. It reduces stress and negativity, and releases feel-good hormones. Ultimately, compassion helps us feel more fulfilled and brings us to a joyful state of being.

GENEROSITY

We typically think of generosity as giving money or other gifts to people or organizations, and that is certainly part of it. But it also involves giving our time, which is our most valuable resource. I've encountered many people who spend a lot of their time and talents helping others, without any expectation of something in return, and they seem so happy. That's because giving really is better than receiving. It brings us joy, and the satisfaction of knowing that we have made a positive difference in the world.

The Cleveland Clinic, in a December 2022 article entitled, "Why Giving is Good for Your Health," says research shows that giving can boost your physical and mental health in numerous ways. When you help someone out or give someone a gift, your brain secretes the "feel good" chemicals serotonin, which regulates mood, dopamine, which provides a sense of pleasure, and oxytocin, which creates a sense of connection with others.

The healthcare provider says other benefits of generosity include:

- Decreased blood pressure
- Better heart health
- A longer lifespan
- Reduced stress

Think about all the ways we can be generous. We can drive someone to doctors' appointments, take care of a family's pets and plants while they're away, help someone out with chores, shovel snow at an elderly neighbor's home, visit someone in the hospital, provide free tutoring, hold a door for someone, and on and on. When we give to others, we're often more aware of our own blessings and feel grateful for what we have. Ultimately, being generous can contribute to a sense of purpose and meaning in life.

Realistically, trying to practice all of these pillars all the time is not easy—maybe not even possible. But they do provide a helpful roadmap. We all need more joy in our lives, and we need to try to provide more joy for others if we can. And if we do, it might even make us happy too!

7

MAKE THE
MOST OF CHANGE

The only constant in life is change," a commonly cited quote attributed to the Greek philosopher Heraclitus, sums up well the idea that change is a fundamental part of reality and that everything is in a constant state of flux. We don't really have any idea as we go about our daily lives the amount of activity that's happening around us on multiple levels and on a grand scale.

Consider for a moment that the Earth is spinning on its axis at about 1,000 miles per hour, and orbiting the Sun at an average speed of some 67,000 miles per hour, according to NASA. On top of that, the space agency notes, our solar system, including Earth, is moving at an average speed of around 450,000 miles per hour as it orbits the center of the Milky Way galaxy. As if that's not enough, the universe is expanding at a speed most of us can't even begin to comprehend. So, if you think you're standing still, you're not. At least, not on an astronomical scale. And then of course, there's the movement of time…

As an astronomy enthusiast, I'm fascinated by this kind of stuff.

But the point is, there is a lot of change happening on a constant basis. On a more practical level, there is frequent change in terms of what's happening in our lives. The vast majority of this change is minor.

You might change your morning routine a bit, begin a new hobby, switch to a different coffee shop, take a different route to work, try a new recipe, update your cell phone answering sound, join a club, read a different genre of book than usual, set a new bedtime schedule, etc. These are basically small adjustments in our daily habits or preferences. They don't significantly disrupt our overall lifestyle.

Then there are the bigger life changes. These include things like getting married, having a child, starting a new job, moving to a new city, switching career directions, getting laid off, retiring, losing a loved one, experiencing a serious illness or injury, graduating from high school or college, etc. Sometimes a whole lot of big changes can happen in our lives in a relatively short period of time. I moved into a new apartment, started a new job, got married, saw the birth of my first child, and bought a house—all within a period of just over a year.

At one point in my life, I moved eight times over a period of just four years. No, I wasn't a fugitive of the law or an Army brat. Things just worked out that way—job changes, upgraded apartments, new opportunities.

Change can be jarring. We're comfortable with the status quo, and we can be uncomfortable with change because of a fear of the unknown, a tendency to stick with what's familiar, and a natural aversion to uncertainty. A December 2019 article by the NeuroLeadership Institute, entitled "Why Change is so Hard—and How to Deal with It," notes that "Our brains have evolved to really like certainty, which stems from our basic drive to survive. We have evolved to predict and control our circumstances because doing so optimizes [the] ability to live. When we experience change, our brains can interpret it as a 'threat' or as a 'challenge.'"

We sometimes resist change even when it would be for the better. Maybe we refuse to try a new restaurant even if we are unhappy with our current favorite, or decline to change our diet despite a strong suggestion from the doctor, or stay in an abusive relationship even after being told not to. It might be avoiding learning a new skill because it seems too challenging, or turning down a promotion due to the fear of having additional responsibilities, or declining a move to a new city even if it presents better opportunities.

I resisted getting a mobile phone for many years, even after smartphones became available. Just about everyone I knew had a cellphone, but I stubbornly held my ground until payphones disappeared and I finally bought an iPhone. And the funny thing is I was writing about cellular communications back in the early 1980s, long before most people had even heard of the technology. Go figure.

Leaving our comfort zones is not always easy. Established patterns and habits can be difficult to break. We like familiar routines, even if they are not ideal. They just feel safer and more comfortable. We feel as if we are holding onto control of our lives.

Recently I went for an appointment at the dentist's office and there was a different hygienist than the one I was accustomed to. Later I learned that the regular hygienist had left the practice months earlier. This rattled me for a few moments, maybe because I'm getting older and even more averse to change. Although we were by no means friends, only seeing each other twice a year, I had known the hygienist for more than thirty years. She was familiar, someone who had shared information about her family and asked about mine. I fully expected to see her there when I arrived, but just like that, she had moved on.

When you think about it, we are constantly facing something we naturally resist: change. As a Baby Boomer, I've seen a good amount of change during the various stages of my life, especially in areas such as technology and consumer electronics. When I began my career as a journalist in 1980, I used a typewriter and paper to write articles, and a rotary dial, desktop telephone to call people for interviews. When I was out of the office on an assignment or covering an event, I relied on payphones to communicate.

There were no personal computers, laptops, or cell phones. There was no Internet, email, or social media. From a technology standpoint, it was not much different than if I had been working in the 1890s. At home, electronic entertainment included listening to vinyl records (before we advanced to cassette tapes) and transistor radios. There were seven television stations to choose from. When color TVs first came out, it was a big deal, as was the arrival of cable, and the early remote controls and video games were primitive compared with today's.

There was no Spotify, no streaming channels, no eBooks. I know it's cliché and makes me sound like an old man to say, "Life was simpler back in the day," but it really was! Still, I've learned over time that we need to make the most of change whenever possible. This is true even when the reason for change is difficult to accept or fully comprehend.

When I was eleven years old, I went on a trip to Italy with my grandmother and my older sister Karen, who was fifteen at the time. While we were in Rome at the beginning of the trip, my grandmother suffered a debilitating stroke. This was a situation we obviously didn't expect, and it changed things dramatically.

I was frightened and didn't fully understand what was happening but, fortunately, we had plenty of family living in the country and they took good care of my sister and me. My grandmother was treated in a hospital in Rome and we took a train to Venice and eventually to San Daniele, the town in Northern Italy where my dad was born. There, we stayed at the large farmhouse belonging to one of my father's uncles, his wife, and their two grown children. It was a bucolic setting, with a great view of the Alps in the distance. This was a new and fascinating experience for me and I tried to make the most of it while my parents back home in the U.S. tried to figure out how and when to get my sister and me home.

We explored the old village where my mother also had family, and met relatives who were fascinated to encounter an American boy and girl. This was the summer of 1969, when men from my country had landed on the moon. Whenever I'd meet someone new and they'd learn where I was from, they would say, *"Luna! Luna!"* the Italian word for moon. We stayed long enough in San Daniele for me to learn quite a few Italian words, sufficient to carry on limited conversations with the natives.

To this day, I don't regret going on the trip. I certainly wish things had gone differently and that my grandmother hadn't gotten sick, but this might have been the chance of a lifetime to see the place where both of my parents had roots. I made the most out of a difficult situation.

I've tried to do the same throughout my working life. In fact, three significant developments in my professional life, each initially jarring experiences, have shaped my career as a writer. The first happened when I was just beginning my career, shortly after I graduated from college with a degree in journalism. I had wanted to be a newspaper reporter in the worst way. I was intrigued by the idea of investigative reporting and turning out exclusive articles that would have an impact on readers. I mailed out query letters to dozens of city newspapers around the country, with no luck.

I decided to move back to my parents' home on Long Island to look for a job. I was depressed and discouraged, and even briefly questioned my decision to major in journalism rather than something more practical. But my dream of working for a big-time newspaper was still alive, and while in the area I thought I'd stop by the offices of *Newsday*, the local paper and one of the largest in the country.

While I was a student at the University of Maryland, I had been fortunate to land an internship at *Newsday* and spent the summer between my junior and senior years covering stories just like the veteran reporters. I enjoyed the thrill of seeing my articles and my byline in the same newspaper I had delivered around my neighborhood as a boy. So I went to the *Newsday* offices to ask for a job. I knew it was a longshot but figured I had nothing to lose.

After some small talk with one of my editors from the internship days, I bluntly asked for a job. And he just as bluntly told me I'd first need to get at least five years' experience as a reporter on a small or medium-sized paper. He also suggested I look into trade journalism, which focuses on writing about specific industries or sectors and covering news and developments that affect professionals in their fields.

I took his advice, and soon after got a job with a magazine covering the some of the "state-of-the-art" business technologies of the day. And this way—by happenstance—I was thrust into an opportunity to write about the "information age" just as it was entering its formative years. It has turned out to be an immense blessing, as I have been able to cover one of the most exciting fields—one that not only encompasses business but every aspect of life. This is a case where the constant change has been a good thing, both from the standpoint of what I write about and the technology I use in my job.

This job led to another, at CMP, one of the fastest-growing technology publishing companies at that time. I spent four years there, learning about many aspects of computer technology. Several years later, I went to work for a newsletter covering the consumer electronics industry, which brings me to the second example. I'd been at this job for about four years when one morning my boss called me into his office, which he often did at the start of the week, to discuss stories we would work on for that week's issue.

I had recently begun needing dialysis treatments because of kidney failure, and he knew this. After he asked me what was happening with regard to my getting a kidney transplant and I told him I was planning to get on a waiting list soon, he gently but directly told me I was being laid off because the company needed to make changes. I was stunned, and then angry, because of the way he worded things, which made it sound like I was being fired because of a health condition. I had never been fired before and was feeling all kinds of emotions: fear, anger, frustration, humiliation.

When I called Reneé to give her the news, she was surprised but handled it much more calmly than I had. "We'll be okay," she tried to assure me. "This is a setback but it's not the end of the world." I was relieved at her reaction. She could have panicked and that would have made things even worse. If Reneé was as worried as I was about our financial prospects, she wasn't showing it. "I'll bet this turns out to be a blessing in disguise," she predicted. "This will lead to something better. You watch."

It took a bit of time and effort, but her prediction proved to be correct. Within about six months I began freelancing for CMP, the company I had worked for prior to taking the job with the newsletter company. Within a few months I was hired to a full-time job on one of CMP's up-and-coming magazines. I thrived in this atmosphere, working with other young editors and frequently landing cover stories. I enjoyed getting back into writing for a publication that covered subjects I found interesting.

Eventually, I was put in charge of one of the magazine's special issues, one of which became the largest issue the magazine had ever produced. This gave me immense satisfaction. Reneé had no idea how right she was when she said losing my job in the city was a blessing in disguise.

The third event that changed the course of my career was one I described a bit in the previous chapter, when I lost the job at CMP and began my time as a freelancer. While it was initially a shock and I occasionally miss the camaraderie of working in an office with lots of other people, I know that I'm much better off as a freelancer and it has enabled me to have success.

It was following that layoff that I also wrote my first book, *New Life*, about organ transplant recipients. Being my own boss and being able to work from home has been a blessing, especially given the health issues I've experienced. All three of these changes were initially stunning and devastating. I felt lost, defeated, perplexed. But each time I was able to find a new and better direction. No matter how bleak things might appear, there are always new possibilities on the horizon. Never give in to despair.

One final example stands out in my mind about making the most of change. When the world was brought to a virtual standstill by the Covid pandemic, all kinds of plans got scuttled. We were all forced to change many facets of our lives, seemingly overnight. At the beginning of 2020, I had lofty goals of traveling to Yellowstone National Park, Florida, Southern California, and Hawaii. But with Covid, those plans evaporated.

Because I'm immunocompromised and more susceptible to viruses, the travel ban for me extended even beyond the availability of vaccines and boosters. I knew it wouldn't be wise for me to be hanging around in airports and hotels or on planes, even with a mask on. Naturally, I was disappointed by these limitations. But then it occurred to me that since we couldn't travel out of town, why not visit local places near our home on Long Island? We did and, as a result, discovered a treasure trove of parks, trails, preserves, and wildlife refuges we didn't even know existed.

We went on to visit more than a dozen of these places over the next few years. We got to enjoy beautiful views of the Atlantic Ocean and the Long Island Sound. We saw rivers, streams, brooks, and an array of wildlife creatures, plants, and flowers. I've lived in this area most of my life and have visited many interesting places, including outdoor attractions. But I was not aware of many of the places we visited following the Covid travel ban. It turned out to be a blessing in that it helped to open our eyes to wonders that are within an hour or two drive from our home.

A lesson for me here was that it is good to be flexible and open to shifting gears when necessary. Sometimes a new and unexpected roadblock can lead us down new paths, to new adventures that are waiting for us to enjoy. Like most people, I don't like change. But I've learned that some things are out of our control. It's what we do with the "new normal" that matters.

My wife shared this quote with me from quilter and blogger Rachel

Hauser: "Life can always, always surprise you. That doesn't feel like a threat to me, rather more of a curiosity and a promise. Like a book that you want to keep reading, or better, like a story that you are making up as you go. What will happen next year or the next? The only way to find out is to keep on living."

Change is constant. What's important to remember is that you can turn the changes into positives if you put your mind to it.

8

ATTITUDE IS EVERYTHING

When it comes to dealing with things like change, it's our mindset that matters. Attitude—how we respond to ideas, objects, people, or situations—is everything. Though attitude can sometimes have a negative connotation, as in—"That guy's got a real attitude, doesn't he?"—our attitude can be an enormous asset to us, and a source of limitless positivity. And as I discussed in chapter two, positivity is something we all need to strive for.

Attitude is something we can control. It might not seem that way when we're in the midst of a heated argument with our spouse or our boss, or when we face a major crisis like losing a job. But our attitudes, our approaches to how we address what life throws at us, can make all the difference.

When I was a journalism student at the University of Maryland in 1980, I contacted a senior editor at *U.S. News & World Report*. This was not an attempt on my part to get a job at the magazine once I graduated—although the thought did cross my mind and I would have been thrilled with that outcome. Rather, I was requesting to meet with the editor because I had come across an article that said he had received a kidney transplant and was doing well. I had recently learned that I had a kidney disease that most likely would require a transplant at some point, and I wanted to know what the experience was like.

The news that he was doing well was encouraging. Here was someone who had achieved success in my chosen field of journalism and was dealing with kidney failure. I had to meet this man. Figuring I had nothing to lose, I called the editor at his office and explained my situation. He said he was delighted to hear from me and invited me to join him for lunch.

We met at a restaurant in Washington, D.C., not far from his office. I soon learned that despite his health problems, the editor had an upbeat approach to things. He had willed himself to overcome his physical limitations and was making the most out of life. Though I've long forgotten much of the conversation, I do remember him telling me attitude was the most important thing in life. How I felt about and responded to whatever happened to me down the road was what I needed to be concerned about.

The editor said something like, "No matter what happens to you in the future, never give up hope. Look at me. I'm functioning perfectly well with someone else's kidney. Not long ago there was no such thing as dialysis or transplants and I would have died of kidney failure. The key thing is attitude. That's what will get you through this."

That was forty-five years ago, and I've not forgotten that lesson. I think it has helped me get though a number of major setbacks. This was one of the many valuable lessons I've learned from people who had faced or were facing illnesses or other setbacks.

A little more than a year later, I was in a car accident. I never saw it coming. A car hit mine from behind and pushed it into the opposite flow of traffic, where it was struck hard by another car. After I regained consciousness, the paramedics told me that the impact had thrown me from the driver's seat out the passenger window and onto the street. An alert policeman who happened to witness the crash as he was walking out of a diner quickly got me the medical help I needed. Otherwise, I might not have made it. When I arrived at the emergency room, a doctor told me I was lucky to be alive, considering what had happened. I was admitted to the hospital and placed in a room with another patient.

Despite my many injuries, including a concussion and broken collarbone, all I could think and talk about was my car. I had just bought it a month before and now it was a scrap heap. At one point, my roommate said he had overheard what I'd been saying about the car. "Don't be worrying about that, man, it's just glass and metal," he said. He was lying in his bed, and, because there was a curtain between our beds, I couldn't see him. "Insurance will pay for it," he said. "What's important is that you're alive and you're not hurt that bad. It sounds like you had a really close call." He sounded young, maybe in his twenties, and I was irritated by what he said. I wasn't about to take the advice of someone who had no idea what I was going through.

Later, when a nurse pushed back the curtain, I could see the man for the first time. His entire body was covered with bandages except for his face and his left leg, which was in a cast and suspended from his bed. He was indeed young, about my age, I guessed. A nurse later told me he had broken his leg, and while recuperating at home a fire broke out and he was badly burned as he tried to escape the flames.

The man would likely have to spend months in the hospital, and might never walk normally again. I felt bad for thinking the way I had. It was another lesson in life. My attitude changed drastically. I quickly forgot about the car. In fact, I didn't think much about it at all until a month or so later, when I went to the body shop where it was being held.

When I saw the extent of the damage, I was shocked. The front end was crushed like an accordion, the front driver and passenger doors were gone, and all the windows had been shattered. The emergency room doctor—and my wise, young roommate—had been right. I was lucky to be alive.

I have failed many times to take a positive approach to things that have happened to me. But in general, I've been able to bounce back from adversity because I have ultimately not allowed any setbacks or traumas to define me as a person. I've tried to keep in mind that these are things that have happened to me; they are not who I am. I have willed myself—with the help of many, many people over the years—to try to get over whatever hurdle I was facing.

As I mentioned in the first chapter, my initial reaction to losing my left foot was understandably not great. But with some encouragement from Reneé, other family members, the medical staff, and others, I was able to turn my attitude around, accept the realities and get on with life. Learning how to walk with a prosthetic leg would not have been possible had I not shifted to an attitude of acceptance. I told myself I would work hard to regain my walking skills, and I have embraced that attitude to this day.

One of the biggest challenges I've faced was an episode of sudden cardiac arrest in the summer of 2022. Although much of the event is blurry, I remember being disoriented, floating between some fragment of consciousness and a disturbing sleep. I was lying on a stretcher, and a bunch of people were standing over me or moving around the room, some shouting instructions. I felt a lot of pressure on my chest and other strange sensations. There was something covering my mouth and I was struggling to swallow. It all felt like a nightmare I wanted desperately to end.

Later on, as I was recuperating in the hospital, a lot of thoughts were flying around in my mind. This included constant questions about why this had happened. These weren't "why me" questions, but just, why? Why did it happen in the first place when I had just had my cardiac function tested not too long before? Why was a cardiologist who wasn't even supposed to be on call right there in the emergency room to help resuscitate me just when I needed him to be there? And why did I survive—with my cognitive function intact—after being clinically dead for nearly ten minutes?

I wasn't able to get real answers to any of these questions; in fact, to this day I haven't gotten the answers. Regardless, I resolved to take a positive approach to this. I was lucky to be alive. I had become a member of an exclusive group of sudden cardiac arrest survivors. The experience had enabled me to appreciate mortality perhaps better than most people.

Largely because of the cardiac arrest, I try to appreciate whatever time I have left. That includes enjoying and embracing the good moments when they happen. And it also includes experiencing the bad moments and letting them pass. This is what life is: good and bad, happy and sad, optimistic and pessimistic, hopeful and despairing. Our attitude about what happens to us means everything, and fortunately we get to choose how we feel and respond.

On the two-year anniversary of the cardiac arrest, rather than try to forget those horrible moments, I chose to celebrate the day as my second "rebirthday." I realized that those dreadful nightmarish moments were indeed the moments in which the medical staff was bringing me back to life. As I celebrated the second anniversary, I remembered how truly fortunate I was on the day of the arrest because of a series of events. For things to go as they did on that morning makes it all seem like a miracle—and perhaps it was. The survival rate for cardiac arrests is not high. Less than ten percent of people who experience these events outside of a hospital survive, according to the American Heart Association.

Many of the people who do survive suffer from effects such as cognitive impairment. A lot of them are angry or depressed. I have felt that way myself from time to time, which is all the more reason why attitude is so important. And so, on that anniversary day and up until the present, I am grateful for the "extra" time I have received.

Sometimes it can be the more mundane events of everyday life that can impact your attitude. Family, work, social interactions, health, weather, commute, career outlook, personal finances, and many other factors can influence how you feel. Our attitude is often influenced by what we think of ourselves and how we treat ourselves. A lot of us probably put ourselves down and criticize ourselves more than we should, and that can certainly affect our attitude.

Many of us have fallen into the habit of negative self-talk, in which we call ourselves idiots for not understanding something or forgetting to do something. We take blame for things that are not our fault, or not completely our fault. Maybe we regret some action, and berate ourselves with "I never should have" corrections; or we compare ourselves to others, wondering why we can't be as smart, or wealthy, or attractive, or lucky as they are.

Nobody likes a bully. But when you think about it, how many times do you quietly bully yourself in the course of a day? If we don't love ourselves and praise ourselves, how can we have a positive attitude? In a 2018 article for *PositivePsychology*, mental health policy researcher Courtney Ackerman, presented a list of positive attitudes. Here are a few that resonate with me:

- Looking adversity in the eye, and laughing.
- Enjoying the unexpected, even when it's not what you wanted originally.
- Motivating those around you with a positive word.
- Using the power of a smile to reverse the tone of a situation.
- Being friendly to those you don't know.
- Getting back up when you fall down—no matter how many times you fall down.
- Not letting other people's negativity bring you down.
- Being a source of energy that lifts those around you.
- Being happy even when you have little.
- Having a good time even when you are losing.
- Being happy for someone else's success.
- Having a positive future vision, no matter how bad your current circumstances.

Many aspects of your life are out of your control: the weather, the economy, how other people think and behave, how other people treat you, natural disasters such as pandemics, the past and the future, the passage of time. One thing you can control is your attitude, and that can make all the difference in the world as you face a variety of experiences. By adopting the right attitude, you can make a difficult situation more tolerable and a pleasant situation even better.

9

CAPTURE MOMENTS THAT MATTER

We experience so many memorable moments in life: birthdays, anniversaries, holidays, vacation trips, and countless others. But as we journey through life, some of the memories can fade or even be forgotten entirely. Luckily, many of these memorable moments might be tucked away in a shoebox in the attic—or even on your smartphone. We live in a time where taking pictures is probably more prolific than ever. It is estimated that 1.81 trillion photos are taken worldwide each year. That equates to five billion per day or 57,000 per second!

When's the last time you looked through an old photo album or scrolled through some of the thousands of pictures on your phone? Whether it's newer photos or older ones, these images give you a chance to revisit moments you have experienced in your life. Many of them are precious moments spent with loved ones and friends who are no longer here, or who have moved far away.

I've long been fascinated by photography. When I was a teenager, I created a part-time darkroom in the laundry room in our basement.

My parents very kindly bought me an enlarger—the device that projects an image from a negative onto photographic paper. When I had shot all the pictures on a roll of film in my camera, I would enter the room, which was lit only by a red "safelight" that provided illumination only from parts of the visible spectrum to which the photographic material in use is completely insensitive. This way, I wouldn't expose and ruin the film.

When I closed the door behind me, another light outside the room indicated that I was working in the darkroom, and that no one was to open the door. I would then set up plastic trays that contained the chemicals needed to develop and "fix" the pictures. Then I'd take the roll of undeveloped film and place it in a small developing tank. Once the film was developed into negatives, I would place it in the enlarger and expose an image onto a piece of the special paper for a specific period of time. Next, I would place the paper in the tray with the developing chemical. I can still remember watching with great anticipation as a black and white image slowly emerged on the paper. Using plastic tongs, I'd move the paper to the next tray to fix the image.

Once the process was complete, I would hang the photos up to dry on a mini clothesline conveniently located in the room. Once they had completely dried, I would proudly show off my work to family and friends. I'm actually quite surprised that I remember all this after fifty-plus years. This hobby gave me rudimentary understanding of how photography works—at least photography as it existed in the early 1970s.

My mother has a bunch of photo albums, some with pictures going as far back as the 1920s. I enjoy looking through these from time to time, fascinated by the depictions of relatives and others, many of them long gone. It's fascinating to see how my parents looked when they were young, and the apartment in Queens, New York, they rented when I was a baby. One photo was a rare image of three of my grandparents—the fourth, my mother's father, had passed away the week I was born—along with my family posing in front of our new house in the suburbs.

One of my first jobs was at a publishing company that specialized in producing photography magazines. And while I worked for a publication that covered office technology, I was probably more interested in the photo magazines. These days I delight in posting photos on Instagram and Facebook, mostly nature scenes from local preserves, parks, beaches, and trails that I shot with my iPhone.

I'm sure many of us of a certain age continue to appreciate the great thing about photography and cameras today: you can take countless pictures of someone or something and instantly see the results. I'm old enough to remember when taking pictures meant choosing between using color or black-and-white film and having a limited number of photos you could take with a roll of film. You needed to be very discerning about what to photograph, because a typical roll of film might provide only twenty-four or thirty-six pictures.

After you were done shooting the roll of film, you had to wait to get it developed before seeing your pictures and finding out whether you actually got the shot you wanted. There was definitely an element of excitement and anticipation as you waited to see your pictures, and a thrill when you received the package of photos from the developer. Inevitably, some of the pictures would be disappointing, especially if you completely missed what you really wanted to capture.

Even with a digital camera or smartphone, you can still manage to miss the picture you want to capture. But in general, it is so much easier to photograph people, moments, and places, and get multiple chances to produce the image you want. What has not changed about photography are the opportunities to capture memorable, beautiful, and unique subjects. They are all around us. While artificial intelligence can generate all kinds of images, there's still nothing like capturing the smiling faces of your kids at a theme park, or the antics of your pet dog or cat.

While modern photography might give us instant gratification in getting to see our work, the real value of pictures remains the same: they give us chances to remember and appreciate the people in our lives, the places we have been to, and the experiences we have enjoyed—sometimes years after we've taken the pictures. But when you think about it, how many times do you take pictures on your phone and then quickly forget about them? I know I do this. I've lately tried to take some time to scroll through my photos, to gain a renewed appreciation of the moments of my life that I captured.

When I was creating a photo gallery for my blog site, I took the time to go through nearly 2,000 photos I had taken over the years with my iPhone. In many cases, I hadn't seen these pictures since shortly after taking them. As I looked at the photos, I was reminded of the people and experiences behind them, moments of my life that I had captured and could look back on and enjoy again.

I also recently had the opportunity to go through old photos that were in a box tucked away in a closet. These were the kind of pictures taken the old-fashioned way, with film and printed on paper. Some of these were pictures I took during my college years. There were also some from a cross-country car trip I took when I moved from Northern California to New York in the mid 1980s, and from a business trip I took to East Asia around the same time.

As I looked over the photos from college years, I saw people, dorm rooms, buildings, and scenery that I had not seen or really thought much about in years. This brought back instant memories of those times. I found myself wondering what my college friends are doing these days, where their lives have taken them. I lost touch with them a long time ago, which happens. We get busy with our lives and regular communication turns into sporadic contact and then the connection breaks off all together. Fortunately, we can remember the people in our lives through photos, and this is what I did as I shuffled through the photos of my college chums, often in goofy poses that reflected the fun we had when we weren't busy studying, helped bring those memories back.

The pictures I took from the cross-country road trip reminded of the many places I got to visit along the way. One of the highlights was the Grand Canyon. Although the photos have faded and fail to capture the true splendor of this natural wonder, they did remind me of the time I visited and stood in awe as I looked into the canyon. Other stops on my trip included the Painted Desert, Pikes Peak, and the Gateway Arch. The images instantly brought me back to those places, and reminded me of how lucky I was to take a trip like that in my youth.

The photos from my trip to Asia included scenes of the Great Wall of China, the Forbidden City in Beijing, downtown Tokyo, and the Hong Kong skyline. Sure, I can look at beautiful pictures of all these locations on any number of travel websites or in books. But seeing the pictures I took, many of them faded or out of focus, reminded me that I had been lucky enough to see these places in person.

I was especially fascinated by the shots I took of people in these countries. One is of a group of young Chinese students and their teacher, who happily posed for me in the outskirts of Beijing. And then there were the scenes from places in China I visited that were off the beaten path. This was a time before China had opened itself up to western visitors, so I was quite privileged to be there and capture these moments on film.

If you haven't looked back through your photographs in a long time, the old ones and the new ones, it might be worth it. You can find some great memories waiting to be rediscovered and embraced. Photos can help remind us of the people, places, and things for which we are grateful. They are snapshots in time, frozen images that can come to life in our minds as we think back to when we took them and what we were doing at the time.

In addition to photos, videos can also give us a chance to revisit enjoyable moments of our lives. I remember looking at old Super 8 home movies my father filmed when we were kids. Some were from long-ago vacation trips to places like the Expo '67 World's Fair in Montreal, where my grandmother and two of my uncles and their families lived, or Cape Canaveral, Florida, where I captured a rocket taking off from a launch pad on its way to Mars. Watching these grainy movies was always a thrill. It was like living the moments over again, and seeing them from an entirely different vantage point (if I wasn't the one operating the movie camera).

Later, camcorders, and even later, smartphones, have given us the opportunity to capture scenes from our lives. Maybe it's our kids playing soccer or baseball, or our families celebrating Christmas or enjoying a backyard barbeque—whatever it was the moments were captured. When I watch videos, they instantly bring me back to those moments, whether they were recorded a few years ago or decades in the past.

It's important to note that looking at photos or videos does not need to be a matter of dwelling on the past. Look at it as an opportunity to help count the blessings you have captured over the years. Some might consider looking at photos—especially older ones—an exercise in futility that forces us to view younger, perhaps healthier and happier versions of ourselves. And yes, doing this will not appeal to everyone. But I look at it as a chance to glimpse the joyous moments of our lives, which we can bring to life once again.

There's another way I've found to capture moments of life, although it's a bit off the trail from cameras and phones. In 2011, I took up painting. I paint with acrylics, and nearly all the works I've done are landscapes. Some of my favorite paintings are the ones that depict places we've been to, whether it's the local arboretum or a beach in Hawaii. What adds to the pleasure of enjoying the scenes in the paintings is the fact that I created these images over a period of time. It took time and effort that was well worth it.

You don't have to take up painting—although it can be a relaxing and fulfilling hobby. Anyone with a smart phone or camera can become an artist with the push of a button. Life is precious, and so are the times of our lives. Remember, as you're capturing the moments of your life, to be sure and enjoy them as well.

10

SIT BACK AND ENJOY THE SHOW

Movies give us a chance to escape, to live vicariously through their adventures, or to learn lessons about life we otherwise wouldn't have. I've always enjoyed watching movies. One of my earlier memories is going to see *The Sound of Music* when it came out in 1965 with my maternal grandmother, who was visiting from Montreal.

This was a time before multiplexes, when going to the movies meant sitting in a large theater that had a very big screen. It was a great experience, with uniformed ushers guiding us to whatever seats were available, and an intermission in the middle of the movie that gave viewers a chance to stretch their legs and maybe grab a popcorn or candy snack in the lobby.

Years later, after the multiplexes had pretty much made the older theaters obsolete, I got to visit one of the last remaining traditional theaters. It was 1981, and my childhood friend Steve Borheck and I went to see *Raiders of the Lost Ark* at the RKO Keith's Theater in the Flushing neighborhood of Queens in New York City. The theater was built in 1928, and its interior was elaborately designed in a Spanish Baroque Revival style.

An oval grand foyer led to the double-level auditorium, which had a blue ceiling and gilded-plaster decorations. The theater originally operated as a vaudeville theater, and the screen, as I remember it, was gigantic. I got to experience not only a superb movie that is one of my all-time favorites, but a spectacular venue that unfortunately no longer exists.

In recent years, I've found a new appreciation for films, particularly those that have upbeat, inspirational messages. Because of Covid and a sharp drop in the number of new movies I want to see in the theater, the vast majority of times I've watched movies over the last few years have been on my television at home. It might not be quite the same experience as watching on the big screen, but the sentiments and messages still come through loud and clear.

Following is a list of some of the movies I find particularly inspirational. It's a fairly broad spectrum of movies, crossing over several genres and time periods. Each has a special meaning to me, or influenced me in certain ways. This is by no means an exhaustive list, but these movies (in alphabetical order) are ones I have found to be especially uplifting, motivating, or thought provoking. Many have themes of positivity and gratitude.

BREAKING AWAY (RELEASED IN 1979)

I remember going to see this movie in a theater with friends while I was a student at the University of Maryland. It's a compelling underdog story focused on four working-class friends who have recently graduated from high school and aren't sure what to do with their lives.

The characters are relatable and, for the most part, likable, the acting is good, and the story has humor about class dynamics. *Breaking Away* is a heartwarming journey about a young man grappling with self-doubt, family expectations, and finding his own identity as he pursues his passion.

The film balances some lighthearted moments with emotional depth, so it's funny as well as touching. It was particularly fitting for me personally—and for my friends—given that we were all about the same age as the main characters and were no doubt facing a lot of the same issues.

CASABLANCA (RELEASED IN 1942)

This is a genuine classic and one of my all-time favorites. Among the main themes are loyalty and a willingness to make personal sacrifices for the greater good. In standing up to evil, everyone can make a difference. The film takes place during World War II, and one of the most moving aspects of it are that many of the actors were refugees who had fled Nazi-occupied Europe.

Casablanca has a powerful and relatable story about love and sacrifice set against the backdrop of the war, and features a number of iconic characters. Humphrey Bogart is great as the central character, but really, the acting is excellent all around. The movie has lots of memorable lines that have become a part of popular culture. Even though the story takes place during a time that occurred decades ago, I think its timelessness makes it relatable today. I've watched this movie a number of times and still find it remarkable. There is one stirring scene involving a singing battle that is a movie moment for the ages.

CAST AWAY (RELEASED IN 2000)

Cast Away is about a man, played by Tom Hanks, who struggles with extreme loneliness and desperation on a deserted island. There's a real range of emotions in this story, even though there is hardly any dialogue. Among the main lessons of the movie are perseverance, physical and emotional survival under the most difficult circumstances, resilience, the importance of connection (involving a volleyball named Wilson), and the potential for transformation and exploring new possibilities in life.

Ultimately the man re-evaluates the priorities in his life, and changes from being a workaholic businessman to someone who is deeply introspective and appreciative of the simple things in life.

CODA (RELEASED IN 2021)

CODA, which stands for child of deaf adults, is a story about pursuing a dream despite difficult obstacles. Positive themes include the love of family, empathy for others, and the need for hope. The movie authentically portrays the experiences of a family with deaf parents through the perspective of the hearing child.

The authenticity comes from the great performances by a cast of largely deaf actors, who use American Sign Language to communicate. *CODA* tackles themes such as family dynamics and coming-of-age struggles. It has a heartwarming and emotional narrative. Like other movies on this list, it evokes a range of emotions, from laughter to tears.

FIELD OF DREAMS (RELEASED IN 1989)

I've watched some good baseball movies, and this is one of my favorites. Ultimately about much more than the game, *Field of Dreams* blends fantasy with actual baseball history, covering themes of family reconciliation and confronting past regrets. And all of this takes place in a magical setting—a baseball field in an Iowa cornfield—that features appearances by legendary players such as "Shoeless" Joe Jackson.

I especially like the way a character named Archibald "Moonlight" Graham highlights the importance of pursuing dreams, even if they seem impossible, and finding fulfillment in the unexpected turns of life. The movie has a great cast, and shows us that hearing voices and being illogical can sometimes be a good thing. I'm not ashamed to admit that one scene toward the end of the film invariably brings tears to my eyes—no matter how many times I watch it.

FINDING NEMO (RELEASED IN 2003)

Pixar has made a lot of great movies, and I think this is one of the best. *Finding Nemo,* which takes place mostly underwater, covers themes including the importance of friendship, personal growth, and the need for teamwork and perseverance in overcoming challenges. It shows us why we should embrace the world as it is rather than live in fear.

This is a really compelling story about a father's love for his son, with well-developed characters such as Marlin and Dory. It includes a heartwarming message about overcoming fears and accepting differences, and resonates with audiences of all ages. Like all great movies, *Finding Nemo* evokes emotions. It elicits tears as well as laughs, and has moments of tension and suspense with heartwarming interactions and comedic relief. In my opinion it's the best fish movie since *Jaws* and the *Incredible Mr. Limpet.*

THE GRAPES OF WRATH (RELEASED IN 1940)

The first time I watched this movie was in a high school class, and it had an indelible impact on me. Based on the classic book of the same name, this movie is filled with inspiring messages, delivered by an interesting cast of characters. These messages include overcoming disappointment, false promises, and loss, the importance of being resilient despite extreme hardship, and the need to embrace hope even when things might seem hopeless.

The Grapes of Wrath portrays the plight of Dust Bowl migrants during the Great Depression. It follows the struggles of the Joad family, including the main character played by Henry Fonda. It's a story about hardship, resilience, family bonds, and the endurance of the human spirit in the face of extreme adversity.

HIDDEN FIGURES (RELEASED IN 2016)

I'm a fan of pretty much anything having to do with outer space, so any movie that involves NASA and space travel is likely to appeal to me. But I think this film would resonate with anyone looking to be inspired. *Hidden Figures* presents a fascinating view of three women who overcame gender and racial barriers to help make possible one of the greatest operations in U.S. history: the launch of astronaut John Glenn into orbit.

This is an often overlooked story of these brilliant African American women who played a pivotal role in NASA's early space missions during a time when segregation was still quite common. It showcases their resilience and intelligence, and the impact they had on history while confronting systemic racism. The movie is both inspiring and educational.

HIGH NOON (RELEASED IN 1952)

Another Hollywood classic, this movie covers themes such as courage, integrity, facing up to fears and holding on to principles in the face of overwhelming odds. It has an intense, real-time feel that's built around a ticking clock, a morally conflicted sheriff, and a story that explores areas such as personal responsibility and community apathy. The growing tension leads up to the inevitable confrontation.

Most of us have to struggle with fear and doubt now and then, and this movie shows how the sheriff handles this as he tries to protect his town even as no one else will stand with him.

THE IMITATION GAME (RELEASED IN 2014)

This is an excellent wartime movie about sticking to one's beliefs, even when encountering significant roadblocks. Its message is that we must not let fear or uncertainty keep us from taking necessary risks or living life in the moment.

The compelling story centers on Alan Turing, the brilliant mathematician who played a key role in cracking the German Enigma code during World War II. The movie depicts the tension of the code-breaking mission while also raising questions about ethics. I'm no math whiz, so I was fascinated with this story of people who were able to solve complex cryptography and code-breaking challenges using their skills. Their efforts had a major impact on history.

IT'S A WONDERFUL LIFE (RELEASED IN 1946)

This is another one of my all-time favorite movies. What astounds me is that it did not do all that well at the box office and it was not a critical success when it first came out. Now it's considered by many to be among the greatest films ever made. Despite its dark moments, I think this is one of the most uplifting films ever made, reminding us that our lives are valuable. It tells a powerful story about the importance of patience, sacrifice, community, family, and the positive impact one individual can have on others.

Sometimes we need to stop and think about the good we bring to the world, including in ways we will never know. Unlike George Bailey (played by Jimmy Stewart), we will not likely have angels come down from heaven to give us guidance. But we can remind ourselves of our own worth and what our lives mean to others around us.

THE KARATE KID (RELEASED IN 1984)

This movie was extremely popular when it came out, and it's endearing on multiple levels. It offers a lot of good lessons, including the importance of commitment, respect for others, facing up to fears, and finding balance in life. *The Karate Kid* blends martial arts action with a compelling coming-of-age story. It features a strong mentor-student relationship between Mr. Miyagi and Daniel, with karate lessons serving as metaphors for life lessons about overcoming adversity, and the importance of perseverance and self-discipline.

In the story, the main character is adapting to his move to California from the East Coast and trying to fit in. The movie came out shortly after I moved to California from New York, so I found it all the more relatable—even though I did not take karate lessons. Wax on, wax off.

THE KING'S SPEECH (RELEASED IN 2010)

Even a king can have a physical or emotional disorder—in this case a severe stutter—that gets in the way of performing his duties. This story is about how King George VI learns to trust his speech therapist after a rough start, and how he works hard to overcome this challenge.

It's a compelling story about overcoming personal challenges, making progress through therapy, and the importance of human connection. It took place during a significant historical period in Britain, World War II, which adds drama and tension. One of the key messages I took away is the value of perseverance. We have to keep at it, no matter how difficult the struggle.

OCTOBER SKY (RELEASED IN 1999)

This is yet another space-related movie about a coal miner's son who was inspired by the first Sputnik satellite launch in the 1950s to take up rocketry, against his father's wishes.

It's a heartwarming and inspiring story that's based on a true event about a young boy who overcomes obstacles to pursue his dream of building his own rockets. There's a father-son relationship that evolves from conflict to understanding.

One of the takeaway lessons is that with the right amount of determination and help from friends, we can try to realize our dreams. Despite roadblocks, including perhaps some from within our own families or communities, we need to persevere.

ON GOLDEN POND (RELEASED IN 1981)

On Golden Pond is a heartfelt, emotional movie that features some great actors—Henry Fonda, Katharine Hepburn, and Jane Fonda—at their best. Among the main themes of the movie are the strength of marriage, aging and facing mortality, and repairing long-strained relationships before it's too late.

The idyllic setting, a lake in New England, is part of the charm. I found myself wanting to visit this fictional place, and it does remind me a bit of the lakeside vacation spot in Pennsylvania that my family vacationed at when I was young. Running in contrast to the serene setting is the tension stemming from the family dynamics. This is certainly relatable for many. But overall, it's a thought-provoking film with great performances.

THE RIGHT STUFF (RELEASED IN 1983)

Yes, another space-themed movie. This one, about the early years of America's space program, is a lesson in dealing with dangers, frustrations, and personal crises—and soaring to great heights.

The Right Stuff masterfully captures the spirit of the early space race between the U.S. and the Soviets, focusing on the bravery and sacrifices of the *Mercury* astronauts. Between them and the test pilots who are also part of the story, it's quite a compelling cast of characters and interesting personalities. I remember enjoying the book by the same name prior to seeing the movie. Oftentimes movies don't live up to the books they're based on, but that's not the case here.

ROCKY (RELEASED IN 1976)

This is one of the great underdog stories in the movies. It includes a host of life lessons, including never giving up despite slim odds of success. I think our resilience in the face of challenges helps to define us, and this film does an excellent job of portraying that sentiment.

One of the things that makes this movie appealing to me is that the title character, a small-time boxer struggling to make a go of things, is flawed and vulnerable. It's easy to root for him to succeed. Other great characters help support the narrative that perseverance and determination can help us achieve our goals. *Rocky* also has one of the more inspiring theme songs you'll hear. Makes me want to run up a bunch of steps.

SCHINDLER'S LIST (RELEASED IN 1993)

A powerful, emotional film about the Holocaust, based on a true story, that highlights the triumph of good over unspeakable evil. It includes lessons of unbroken spirit in the face of extreme hardships, and the enormous difference one individual can make. This is a compelling story about redemption, selflessness, and hope.

I had to get a movie directed by Steven Spielberg and with music by John Williams on this list, because they are two of my favorites.

12 ANGRY MEN (RELEASED IN 1957)

This is a truly remarkable film; I would put it in my top five list of all-time favorites. It takes place mostly in a single room and relies heavily on the dialogue and interaction among the twelve jurors deciding the fate of a young man. Each of the jurors has a distinct personality and different motivation.

12 Angry Men shows that even when the odds are heavily stacked against us, we must stick to our principles and not give in to peer pressure. The character development is powerful, and the acting is superb. The way the movie is shot makes you feel like you're in the juror room as the tension builds. I've found it ironic that I like this movie so much even though I'd have no interest in serving on a jury. It is a timeless masterpiece of a film.

TOY STORY 3 (RELEASED IN 2010)

I've enjoyed all of the *Toy Story* movies, but the third installment is my favorite. The main themes are love, friendship, faith, positivity, loyalty, and helping those in need. It's a deeply emotional story about growing up, letting go, and finding new purpose. Although it has the same humor and charm of the earlier movies, it has some serious scenes and an especially powerful ending. I challenge you not to cry.

Toy Story 3 has well-developed characters, poignant scenes, and a suspenseful plot. If you haven't seen the first two *Toy Story* movies, watch them first! We might not watch movies the way we did when we were younger, with the streaming channels replacing the big screens of the theaters as the primary means of viewing, but the power of stories on film to teach us lessons in creative, unique ways, still remains.

BASK IN THE GREAT OUTDOORS

f you're reading this at the beach, on a park bench or picnic blanket, or at some other outside locale, stop for a moment to appreciate what you see around you, the air you're breathing, and the colors of nature. You're fortunate to be enjoying the great outdoors, which can provide benefits you might not even realize.

In my job as a self-employed writer who works from home, I spend a lot of time indoors. That's why I make it a habit to try to go outside as much as I can. I like to walk outside, even if it's just on our backyard patio. Of course, this is easier to do when the weather is nice. But I find that even in the winter, it's good to enjoy the outdoors—even for just a few minutes.

Spending time outside can result in several health benefits, according to a 2022 article on the health information site Healthline by freelance health writer and editor Emily Swaim. These include:

- **Better breathing**. Spending more time in natural green spaces can help lower your risk of respiratory concerns.

You will typically find the freshest air in places with high air circulation, such as an open field.

- **Improved sleep.** Exposing yourself to sunlight can enhance your sleep by helping you feel more tired at night, shortening the time it takes to fall asleep, and improving the quality of your rest.

- **Reduced depression symptoms.** Sunlight can also help ease depression symptoms such as low mood and fatigue.

- **More motivation to exercise.** Working out in green spaces can help boost your motivation to exercise in the future. It offers a nice change of pace from gyms and can make physical activity more interesting and enjoyable.

- **Mental restoration.** Overstimulation from all of your daily screen time and other sources of "noise" can raise your stress levels without you even realizing it. The outside world can offer a mental and emotional refuge.

- **Boosted immune function.** Spending time outdoors can help your immune system function optimally.

- **Protection from short-sightedness.** There is some evidence that spending time outside might help protect against myopia, in part because the outdoors lets your eyes practice looking at objects from various distances.

- **Improved emotional wellbeing.** Spending time outside can help promote emotions such as happiness, peace, and optimism.

Other benefits, according to various research sources, can include increased exposure to Vitamin D from sunlight, reduced anxiety from being in a relaxed environment, opportunities to socialize with others who enjoy being outside, and lower risk of depression.

Some of my best memories of growing up involve being outdoors. Along with my brothers, Steven and Paul, and friends from the neighborhood, I would spend many hours playing baseball or softball on our block. I much preferred playing sports like baseball and hockey with my friends rather than in organized leagues.

Our block was near some horse stables and a farm and, every once in a while, one of the horses would get loose and come trotting down our street, right through our makeshift ballfield. We'd get out of the way and watch in amazement as the horse would go by, followed by a stable hand running down the street to retrieve the stray animal. Then, following the horse delay, we'd get back to our game.

During the summer, there were probably a lot of days when we spent more time outside than inside. It just seemed like a natural way to spend our time. We would go to parks and ride our Stingray bikes to a local candy store to buy licorice and candy sticks. We played tag, hide-and-seek, cops and robbers, and cowboys and Indians. We managed to keep ourselves occupied in one way or another, oftentimes using our imaginations and making up games. As evening approached, we would often hang around by the streetlights, waiting for the ice cream man and chatting the time away until we knew it was finally time to go inside.

When we got older, we played ice hockey on ponds that were mostly frozen or street hockey on parking lots that were mostly empty. Difficult as it might be for modern parents to fathom, ours often had no idea where we were while we basked in the great outdoors for hours and hours. Times certainly have changed. Some time ago, there was a block party on my street. Kids were riding their bikes or scooters up and down the street, playing games with their friends, or just hanging out enjoying the warm weather. They all seemed to be having a great time. But outdoor activities like this, even during the summer, are the exception rather than the rule. Today, many kids are enamored by indoor entertainment options such as video games, smartphones, social media, and other electronic activities.

No surprise, the day following the block party it was quiet on the block. There were no bikes, no games, no sounds of laughter. It was back to normal. And this got me thinking that many of us, not just kids, probably don't go outside as much as we should. Unless we're on vacation, at a ballgame, or at some special occasion, we spend much of our time indoors. Covid certainly lead to an increase in outdoor activities. I recall seeing a lot more people than usual walking around the neighborhood during the lockdowns. But then, over time, this dropped off again.

There are so many options for outdoor activities: parks, trails, beaches, mountains, hills, valleys, campgrounds, lakesides, and preserves. In 2024, Reneé and I were blessed to be able to visit Yellowstone National Park and Grand Teton National Park. The prosthetic leg that I wear enabled me to walk around and visit many of the fascinating places in the parks, with just a few restrictions such as climbing or descending steep inclines. This trip offered some of the most magnificent views of nature I have ever seen or ever hope to see again. We were treated to mountains, rivers, lakes, geysers, hot springs, and waterfalls, and got to see wildlife including bison, elk, coyotes, bald eagles, and beavers.

At one point in Yellowstone, we encountered a large herd of bison crossing one of the main roads. This brought traffic to a standstill and provided us with some wonderful opportunities to snap photos of these creatures. A few of them came right up to our car. I'm grateful for the chance to visit a part of the country that is filled with incredible natural wonders. I appreciate the parks and trails we have near my home on Long Island. But we do not get to experience erupting geysers, roaming bison, or multi-colored hot springs.

One of the most appealing aspects of visiting Yellowstone and Grand Teton was that it allowed us to be mostly off the grid for a few days. The cell service was sporadic at best throughout the parks. This rendered GPS unavailable, which was a bit of a challenge at times. But it also encouraged us to put away our phones, except to take pictures. This helped us to focus more deeply on the wonders that were around us.

Many of us have become highly reliant on our digital devices. We regularly check for emails and texts, scroll through social media feeds, or surf the web. I don't consider myself to be a device addict by any measure. However, to take a break from the digital world, even for a few days, was refreshing.

I can recall times in my life when I was awed by nature. One of my memories of going to college in upstate New York was being awakened in the middle of the night by excited fellow dorm residents because the northern lights, also known as the aurora borealis, were putting on a spectacular display over nearby Lake Ontario. It was breathtaking to watch.

When I lived in Northern California in the 1980s, I would drive along the Pacific Coast Highway now and then, looking down the steep cliffs at the roiling ocean below, and getting out of the car whenever possible to take in the breathtaking sites. I did a lot of exploring around the region, wanting to see as much of the area as I could.

On several weekends I drove out to the old Gold Rush country east of Sacramento, and imagined I was a miner looking for gold in the frontier days.

When it came time to move back east, I elected to take a couple of weeks off from work to drive back so I could see a lot of the country while I had the chance. The drive back to New York took me through some of the most beautiful places I have seen and showed me how remarkably varied this country is. I drove through coastal areas, deserts, valleys, and mountain ranges, stopping at cities along the way including Los Angeles, Las Vegas, Kansas City, and St. Louis. Again, whenever I could, I'd get out of the car and spend a lot of time taking in the scenery outside.

One of the most impressive places I stopped at was the Grand Canyon in Arizona. It's difficult to describe this place because there's really nothing that I've seen that's quite like it. It is a magnificent wonder of nature that's impossible to look at and not be profoundly affected.

The hundreds of miles I traveled took me through the majestic Rocky Mountains, big cities and small towns, and seemingly endless acres of farmland. Along the way there was some snow, rain, tornadoes, and a hailstorm, but for most of the trip there was brilliant sunshine and blue skies.

I've had the good fortune to visit Hawaii several times, including my honeymoon. Reneé and I spent time on the island of Oahu, and I remember fondly the two of us walking hand-in-hand along Waikiki Beach at night, looking up at the stars and feeling the warm water of the Pacific Ocean at our feet. We also visited the beautiful, idyllic Island of Kauai, with lush green gardens, scenic waterfalls, and so many secluded beaches and coves to explore. At night it was so dark that we could see even more stars than we could on Oahu. On a later trip we visited the island of Maui, which treated us to some magnificent scenery and indescribably beautiful beaches.

Much closer to home is another one of my favorite places, Cooperstown, N.Y. Best known for the Baseball Hall of Fame, it is about as bucolic a location as you could find. Tucked away in upstate New York, the village is next to beautiful Lake Otsego, called "Glimmerglass" by the Native Americans who lived in the area. As soon as you arrive, there is a warm, welcoming feeling. It's as if time has stood still and the place is the same as it was years earlier when, as legend has it, Abner Doubleday invented the game of baseball. I've been to Cooperstown a few times and almost wanted to move there once. There's a boat tour around the lake, and it offers beautiful views of the area.

One other place I'd like to mention in this mini-travelogue is Lancaster County, Pennsylvania. Our family took many trips to this area as our sons were growing up, and it made an indelible impression on me. It's known for its Amish community, historic Lancaster city, and countryside. Located off the beaten path in the Amish country, the scenery there is picturesque and pastoral, with rolling hills, farms, and horse-drawn buggies. Standing by a roadside in the midst of all this provided the most serene feeling. It might as well have been two centuries earlier, when people spent a lot more time outdoors than we do in modern times.

On our first trip to this area, during a time when I was relying on dialysis and not in optimal health, we took an old-fashioned train ride on one of the oldest railroads in the country. The scenery was beautiful, with hills and fields of golden corn and lush green pastures all around. It was a marvelous escape from work and health concerns. I felt serene, at peace. Appropriately, the train stopped in a small town called Paradise.

I've chosen these seemingly random examples to illustrate the fact that being outdoors—for whatever reason—can be exhilarating. And enjoying the outdoors doesn't have to mean traveling to exotic places. Your own backyard or a local park can offer a place for solace, relaxation, and recharging.

Many nights I go outside to watch sunsets or look up at the stars. This gives me a different perspective of the world that helps offset any worries or anxieties that might be affecting me at the moment. I never tire of watching the International Space Station move across the sky on a clear night, or looking at the moon and planets. If you're looking for ideas of things to do outside, here are some suggestions:

- Hiking
- Gardening
- Nature photography
- Camping
- Stargazing
- Birdwatching
- Biking
- Picnicking
- Kite flying
- Running
- Exploring nature trails
- Fishing
- Swimming
- Painting

- Skiing or snowboarding
- Playing sports
- Shopping at a farmers' market
- Meditating
- Visiting a flea market
- Miniature golfing
- Kayaking
- Rock climbing
- Ice skating
- Sunbathing

When you think about it, most of our world exists outside our homes and offices, and it's filled with natural beauty. We all need to spend more time enjoying this gift, appreciating the great outdoors and all that it has to offer. As Ralph Waldo Emerson wrote in his poem, "Merlin's Song", we should, "live in the sunshine, swim in the sea, drink the wild air's salubrity."

12

LIVE IN THE MOMENT

You've probably heard the phrase "living in the moment" or the term "mindfulness" in your travels. The idea of paying attention to your present experiences rather than getting caught up in stressful and upsetting thoughts has certainly caught on, and there is no shortage of mindfulness classes and workshops offered by universities, mental healthcare organizations, and others. This is not surprising, considering we live in a world that can be filled with stressful situations. We can have stress at work, at school, and in our homes. Sometimes the level of stress can be overwhelming, and a practice of living in the moment can help.

Research shows that mindfulness—being aware of your surroundings and body in the present moment—can have a multitude of benefits. These include lower levels of stress, decreased depression, improved memory, and strengthened relationships, among others. And the practice of mindfulness does not necessarily require meditation. It's a broader concept of being aware of the moment.

As Jon Kabat-Zinn, professor emeritus of medicine and the creator of the Stress Reduction Clinic and the Center for Mindfulness in Medicine, Health Care, and Society at the University of Massachusetts

Medical School says: "Mindfulness practice means that we commit fully in each moment to be present; inviting ourselves to interface with this moment in full awareness, with the intention to embody as best we can an orientation of calmness, mindfulness, and equanimity right here and right now."

It all sounds great, but living in the moment can be a challenge. Sometimes focusing on being aware of our thoughts, feelings, and surroundings in the current moment, rather than dwelling on the past or anticipating the future, is not easy. Your mind can easily drift toward something that happened in the distant or recent past, maybe something that was hurtful, frustrating, or disappointing. Or perhaps you're focused on a difficult task that you will have to take on in a few weeks.

RocheMartin, an organization that provides tools and services in emotional intelligence, mindfulness, and leadership, has come up with fifty tips for practicing mindfulness. I've included below a few that resonate with me.

- **Practice relaxed attention**. Regardless of how you are feeling—frustrated, bored, sad, irritated, angry—give relaxed attention to the emotion, as if you were watching another person. This can help you become calm.

- **Keep a daily journal**. You can make it a routine to begin your day by writing down some notes about how you're feeling or what's going on in your life. I keep a gratitude journal, making note of the people and things that I'm thankful to have in my life.

- **Repeat a positive affirmation**. It's so easy for us to begin thinking in negative ways. Annoyances are prolific. One way to reverse this is to repeat a positive affirmation such as "I've got this." By repeating the affirmation, you can feel more positive.

- **Listen to people.** I sometimes struggle with this because I get easily distracted or I'm focused on something I'm going to say. Everyone can have something interesting, or even uninteresting, to communicate. By truly listening to what someone else is saying, we can be more focused on the moment.

- **Practice breathing exercises.** Focusing on breathing is one of the most commonly mentioned ways to be mindful. It's an excellent way to calm yourself down when you're feeling stressed, frightened, or angry.

- **Walk.** I find that walking can be a great opportunity to be mindful. If I focus on each step and be aware of the distance I'm going, it can make the walk more purposeful. If I'm walking on a trail or in a park I try to appreciate what I see around me.

- **Slow down.** Whatever you are doing or wherever you are going, slow down and let yourself become more aware of the journey. I sometimes have a tendency to look ahead and therefore not experience the moment fully. We could all benefit by not racing through life.

- **Get back to nature.** I really like this one because I'm enthralled by the natural world. I find that getting out in nature, whether it's a park or trail or even my own yard, can be extremely relaxing. That's especially true if I take the time to appreciate what's around me.

- **Listen to music.** This is another activity that can be very calming. To help me appreciate music I'm listening to on my headphones, I sometimes try to guess or discern which type of instruments the artists are playing. It gives me a greater appreciation for the work that went into composing the piece.

- **Embrace new experiences.** I think we tend to live in the moment more when we're doing something we've never tried before or learning something new. We're kind of forced to automatically focus on what we're doing because it's something new for our brains to process.

Sometimes it's easier to live in the moment than others. In one instance, I was at the Walt Disney World theme park in Florida, which we were visiting on a family vacation. We went to an attraction called Mickey's PhilharMagic, an animated show with astounding 3D effects shown on a large, wraparound screen. It includes the use of water sprays, scents, air puffs, and a variety of lighting techniques, all designed to immerse audiences in a musical adventure.

I'm a child at heart, and this kind of thing might not appeal to everyone. But I was completely enthralled watching the twelve-minute show, waiting for the next thing or character to jump out at me from the screen. At one point, I felt like I was flying along on a magic carpet. This was an escape from reality, but it felt as real as anything I've experienced. I could easily cite a dozen other examples from the Disney parks, including some thrill rides, but I'll leave it with this one.

Another experience that had me thoroughly living in the moment was attending a concert by the Boston Pops. My family and I were sitting in balcony seats just in front of the stage in the concert hall, so we could look down and see the musicians directly below us. The brilliant film composer John Williams was conducting the orchestra as it played music from some of my favorite movies, like *Star Wars*, *Jurassic Park*, and *Raiders of the Lost Ark*. To hear the familiar music and see the musicians playing it right in front of us was a spectacular, unforgettable experience.

When I was a child, I used to occasionally visit my paternal grandmother, who lived in Greenwich Village in New York City. This was the 1960s, when the Village, including its famous Washington Square Park, was the hub of art, music, politics, and literature. It attracted an array of artists, poets, folk singers, and others from all over the United States. It also drew a good number of protesters and activists.

I was a bit too young to fully understand or appreciate all of that, but I did appreciate the view from the roof of my grandmother's apartment building. It wasn't an especially tall building by New York City standards, sixteen stories, but to an eight-year-old boy from the suburbs it was breathtaking. Looking down at the streets, cars, and people below, I was on top of the world, completely focused on the moment.

Around that same time, my dad took us to the Ringling Brothers circus at Madison Square Garden in the city. I remember watching the action in the three rings, trying not to miss anything and thoroughly enjoying the show. He had bought some souvenir plastic devices that would light up at the end and we would swing these around in the air along with many of the other guests. Years later, I went to the same circus at Nassau Coliseum on Long Island with my family, and was just as enthralled as I had been when I was a kid, decades earlier. My complete focus was on what was in front of me.

One other time I was completely immersed in my surroundings happened at Yankee Stadium in the Bronx in New York in May

1998. David Wells, the Yankee's pitcher, was in the midst of throwing a perfect game—no hits, walks, hit batters, or errors through all nine innings. It's an extremely rare feat, occurring about once every 9,900 games. In 154 years of major league baseball history and more than 230,000 games played, there have only been twenty-four official perfect games. I attended the game with my son Andrew, who was ten years old at the time. We were sitting not too far from where the final out of the historic game was made. It was one of my most memorable moments, and I remember being transfixed by the action on the field, totally focused.

Now that I think about it, there are probably dozens, maybe hundreds or thousands—if my memory was that good—of other examples I can come up with where I was truly in the moment. During those times, as far as I was concerned, there was no past and no future, only that exact moment in time to enjoy and embrace. I think the common thread among these examples I shared is that I tried to fully appreciate what was happening at the moment. As far as was possible, I didn't allow my mind to drift to everyday concerns or to events that had happened before or might happen later. The now was all that mattered.

One good reason to fully embrace certain moments is that we don't know when or if that type of moment will ever happen again. Years ago, when I was moving to California, I flew out to Silicon Valley from my home in New York to look for an apartment. On the night I was to head back east, I went to dinner with an aunt who lived in the area, and another relative and his wife, who were on their honeymoon.

It was a nice dinner at a nice restaurant. The company was pleasant, and I enjoyed myself. The young man, a son of my father's cousin, and his new wife were sweet and friendly. Unfortunately, I wasn't completely engaged in the moment. I was thinking ahead to returning my rental car and catching my red-eye flight back to New York. At some point, I got up and said goodbye, then headed up to San Francisco International Airport. As it turns out, I've not seen the young couple since that time we had dinner. They settled somewhere in the Midwest and the opportunity has never presented itself. This was a chance meeting with all of us crossing paths at a particular moment.

Fortunately, I remember the event and the emotions, if not the faces. The lesson is, some people might drop into our lives for just a very short period of time—a passing moment in the span of a lifetime—and we need to treasure and fully embrace those moments while they are happening.

Part of living in the moment is not taking things for granted. Things that happen around us can be so fleeting. I remember when I was in grade school during recess we would do something called "flipping" baseball cards. There were multiple ways of doing this. In one version, two or more opponents would stand a certain distance from a wall, and each flip a card with a flick of the wrist. Whoever got his card closest to the wall won the cards. Another version was to flip your card as far as you could, and whoever's card went the farthest won.

Regardless of how we played it, the object was to win as many cards as possible to add to your collection, even if they got damaged during the flipping events. Then, inexplicably, near the end of the school year many of us would do something we called "flipouts." We would take a huge wad of our baseball cards and throw them into the air and then watch as schoolmates would frantically and deliriously scramble to gather up the cards.

These schoolyard activities seem bizarre now, especially since many of those same baseball cards are worth a small fortune. But they remind me of how things can be fleeting—in this case the games of flipping and the value of the cards themselves. Moments come and go, just like those tattered and bent baseball cards. The fact that I'm still recalling these events fondly more than fifty years later means it had meaning. Perhaps I was living deeply in the moments, as they were happening.

I did revive my interest in card collecting long after these school times. In the early 1990s the collectible card market was booming and I had a great time taking my son Andrew to card shows. Many of the cards on display on the vendors' tables at these events were the same ones my friends and I had enjoyed flipping and hurling skyward when we felt inclined years earlier.

Ever since I experienced the cardiac arrest a few years ago, I've been more aware of the need to live in the moment. I'll never forget when one of the doctors came into my hospital room to give us an update. He kept using the phrase "when you died," and at one point, I interrupted him and asked why he kept saying that. He simply replied, "Well, because that's what happened." It was a bit chilling, and a stark reminder of my mortality. Life can be difficult because of the many worries and distractions life brings, but I keep trying to appreciate the precious moments I have, recognizing that every one of them is a gift.

Living in the moment takes a lot of practice. It requires a conscious effort on our part to focus on the present rather than dwelling on the past or worrying about the future. We need to make mindfulness a way of life. Practicing it daily is the way to get there. And the effort will be well worth it. We all need to remind ourselves that this moment, right now, is the only reality we have. And we need to try to fully appreciate it with whole hearts—and minds.

13

EMBRACE OBSTACLES AS OPPORTUNITIES FOR GROWTH

Everyone faces obstacles in life. Sure, some have it easier than others. I know of people who have lived into their nineties and were hardly ever sick and rarely had to go to the hospital. But experiencing life typically means having to get over hurdles now and then. Even those who might appear to be living a carefree existence could be experiencing an inner turmoil that we can't imagine. In our interactions with people, we need to always assume and acknowledge that others have had to overcome problems, just like we have.

I've had to deal with a number of health issues, some of which I've covered in previous chapters. Each has been an obstacle in its own way. The first time I learned that I had a serious illness threw my very ordinary life into something of a turmoil. It came when I read a letter that a specialist had written to my family doctor. The letter was short and to the point; a straight-forward, emotionless communication from one medical professional to another. It briefly stated that tests I had undergone showed that I had polycystic kidney disease (PKD), a little-known but fairly common, usually hereditary condition in which the kidney tissue is slowly destroyed by fluid-filled cysts. There is no known cure.

This, of course, was devastating news. It was December 1979 and I was twenty-one years old, home from college for the holiday break. Until that day, probably the worst medical problem I had faced was chicken pox. My family, including my parents, older sister, and two younger brothers, was fortunate in that we all enjoyed good health. I was never really exposed to serious illnesses or death, except for what I'd seen in the movies or on television. I had been too young to remember the deaths of my two grandfathers.

Nothing in my experience had prepared me for this startling news of my own illness. Before it happened, I never thought much about medicines, doctors, nurses, or hospitals. Why should I? I was a healthy young man with likely many decades of life to enjoy.

In the days following the startling diagnosis I walked around in a daze, trying to process the situation. I kept my feelings to myself, which was in keeping with my character. I was—and for the most part still am—a private person who keeps most things to myself. But I did ask myself a lot of questions. How could this happen to me? Why me? Why now?

My parents were also devastated by the news. They had a particularly hard time dealing with it because neither one of them appeared to have the disease, even though, in most cases, it's hereditary. For the time being, there seemed to be a dark cloud over the horizon, when only a short time before there was a lot of anticipation and hope about the future.

By the time I returned to my studies at the University of Maryland in January, the shock had worn off somewhat. I was distracted by classes and thoughts of graduation and looking for a job in the spring. Still, I knew that life would never be quite the same. What helped in a big way was when my kidney doctor told me that, for the time being, they would treat my blood pressure and I was to otherwise go on with my life, start a career and a family. I was not to overwhelm myself with this.

Looking back, I realize how great that advice was. I did go on with my life, start a career and a family. I refused to let kidney disease define me, but instead saw it as merely an obstacle to overcome. I'm one of the lucky ones because I was ultimately able to receive a kidney transplant, from my wife, which vastly improved my health and has enabled me to live a relatively normal life. The transplant took place nearly thirty years ago. Talk about a blessing!

Overcoming obstacles takes effort, but it's how we cope with life's challenges. Sometimes it takes mind over matter—controlling a physical condition or other problem by using the mind.

In 2024, I underwent major surgery to fix an internal bleeding issue. The operation was a success, but the recovery process was long and difficult. The complications were not expected, and they delayed my recuperation. At times, I regretted having the surgery at all, feeling drained and discouraged.

Once again, Reneé came to my rescue, encouraging me to fight on. In the midst of the various post-surgical ups and downs, she suggested that I adopt a mantra: "This is tough, but I'm tougher." At first, I didn't think this would help. But I began saying the words to myself and then out loud, and I found that it did help. Just by thinking about the words as I said them, I was able to give myself some assurance that I could get through the challenges. It didn't directly stop the pain or provide me with physical strength, but it did provide me with the motivation to carry on and fight through the challenges.

During this time, I also did a lot of praying. Aside from bringing us closer to God, prayer can offer benefits such as gaining a sense of purpose and meaning, elevating mood, helping to cope with difficulties, enhancing gratitude, promoting mindfulness, and boosting physical healing. And I tried to look for any positive vibes wherever I could find them. Small acts of kindness by the medical staff, texts with good wishes from family and friends, taking tentative steps in the hospital hallways to help with my recuperation, and listening to music on my headphones.

My sister-in-law, Denise Fergusson, began sending me greeting cards on a regular basis, each one with a positive message to promote healing and wellbeing. As the weeks went on, I continued to recover. The experience has not been easy and I still have struggles. But without the coping mechanisms I'm sure it would be far more difficult to deal with.

State of mind is so important. Life sometimes isn't easy, and when we are physically, mentally, and spiritually distressed sometimes it just takes sheer determination and willpower to cope. It might be just a matter of waking up in the morning, getting out of bed and doing the best you can despite whatever challenges you are facing. We need to push ourselves, but always with a gentle reminder that we can only do what we are capable of doing at a given time.

A mental health provider gave me some suggestions for how to make the recovery easier, and I have found these to be helpful: Find comforting and enjoyable things to do; get the proper nourishment you need for healing; draw from your gifts of resilience and coping skills, remembering how you have overcome challenges in the past;

be patient, as this is a temporary setback; be kind to yourself, acting as a coach with your best interests in mind; and think about things to look forward to when you have recovered.

If you are going through a difficult challenge, whether it's a health issue, work problem, family matter, or something else, try not to get discouraged. As hard as it might be, look at the many positives in your life. They are out there, or they are in your heart and mind waiting to be rediscovered.

Here are some tips for dealing with life's obstacles that I've gathered from various sources and from firsthand experience:

- **Make self-care a priority.** Any time of your life, but especially when you are going through a difficult time, it's vital to eat a balanced diet, get enough sleep, and take part in activities that bring you joy. By taking care of your physical and mental health, you can become more resilient and better cope with difficulties.

- **Believe in yourself.** Have faith in your ability to overcome the challenge(s) you are facing. Be confident that you are capable of finding the solutions you need. As I mentioned, attitude is everything. Focus on the successes and progress you have made and reinforce the idea that things will get better.

- **Try to stay positive.** It might not be easy, but don't dwell on whatever is troubling you. It's better to focus on finding solutions and moving forward than to fall into self-pity or a defeatist attitude. Keep in mind that challenges can help you grow. Practicing gratitude can also help promote a sense of positivity. Think of the people and things in your life for which to be thankful.

- **Get help when you need it.** When you're really struggling, don't hesitate to ask for help from your spouse or partner, other family members, friends, a support group, or a mental health professional. People appreciate being needed and trusted, so reach out to others for support and guidance. This gives you an opportunity to share what you are feeling and experiences, which in itself can help you deal with challenges.

In my experience, one of the best ways to overcome obstacles is to use humor. Sometimes I try to evoke thoughts of funny things I have experienced. Years ago, I was going out for a night on the town with a friend of mine and, on the way, we stopped at a bank because he wanted to get some cash. I parked across the street from the bank and my friend went in to make his withdrawal.

While he was in the bank, I noticed a car that looked similar to mine pull up behind me. Moments later, my friend came hustling out of the bank and promptly hopped into the passenger seat of the car behind me. I began laughing hysterically, in part because it was a good ten seconds or more before he realized his mistake. As I watched the spectacle unfold through my rearview window, I tried to imagine what was going through the mind of the driver as a total stranger came running out of a bank and jumped into his car. Once my flustered friend got into my car, I asked him why it took him so long to realize he'd gotten into the wrong car. He said he didn't notice he was in a different car with a different driver. He actually said to the guy, "Okay, let's go, Bob."

This got me laughing hysterically all over again. It was one of those moments that has lived on in my memory and I hope always will, because it's a source of humor, and we all need that from time to time.

Laughter can truly be contagious. If something's really funny, it's hard not to laugh, and when we laugh we naturally feel better. Humor can help us get through obstacles or at least help us deal with them. The benefits of laughter have been well documented. They include decreased levels of stress, stronger immune system, pain relief, lower blood pressure, improved heart health, stronger social bonds, and better mental health. I've tried to use humor even when in the midst of serious health situations because I find it helps to break the tension.

There was a time I needed a metal plate implant to repair a stress fracture of my hip. Unfortunately, the hip specialist at the orthopedic practice I went to was away, so I would be operated on by a doctor who specialized in hand injuries. I was wheeled into an operating room and given a local anesthesia, an epidural similar to what many women receive when they're in labor. They also gave me some Valium to relax me.

After a few moments, I had no feeling in my legs and the doctors got to work. I could hear them referring to some sort of guidebook they were reading about how to do this particular procedure. So they were essentially learning on the job. During the next hour or so, the operating room was seemingly transformed into a workshop. I heard what sounded like a power drill, and then a saw, and then hammering, and then more drilling. Along with this noise came the occasional turning of pages in the manual as they worked through each step.

I could feel no pain as they went about their work, but I did feel a bit of empathy for them because this was clearly not their specialty. Feeling giddy from the Valium and wanting to ease their tension, I said, "Hey, guys, we need some work done at our house. Do you do kitchens?" The surgeon and his assistant laughed and I'm sure appreciated the humor. Lightening things up can sometimes help us overcome obstacles, even those that seem overwhelming at first.

While we're on the topic of humor… As I mentioned, I'm a fan of dad jokes. I enjoy hearing them and telling them. So I'll close with a few. Feel free to chuckle or groan.

Which days are the strongest? Saturday and Sunday. The rest are weekdays.

My friend was showing me his tool shed and pointed to a ladder. "That's my stepladder," he said. "I never knew my real ladder."

Two jumper cables walk into a bar. One of them says, "We'd like a couple of beers, please." The bartender says, "Okay, but don't start anything."

Question: If April showers bring May flowers, what do May flowers bring?

Answer: Pilgrims.

What did the janitor say when he jumped out of the closet? "Supplies!"

Did you hear about the restaurant on the moon? Great food, no atmosphere.

14

LEARN TO TRUST OTHERS

B ack in my college days, I had a summer job working in the mailroom at a big-time New York City corporate law firm. I used to make all kinds of deliveries, within the firm offices and outside. One such errand involved bringing a package of cash—several thousands of dollars—to a bank or another firm. One of the supervisors half-jokingly, and in his gruff voice, told me to act casually while I transported the money, so as not to look conspicuous and possibly get mugged on the way. So I went so far as to toss the package up and down while waiting for elevators or standing on the subway platform waiting for a train.

Looking back, it's a wonder that the managers of the mailroom trusted me with all that money. It probably amounted to way more than I would get paid for the entire summer. For all they knew, I could have hidden the money or given it to a friend to hold, and then made up some story about why I didn't get the money to its destination. Of course, I would never have done these things. But they couldn't have known that for sure. They trusted me based on

my previous behavior and performance as a mailroom delivery boy—
and what they perceived to be my good character.

Trust can be a complex thing, and yet we rely on it so much in
our day-to-day lives. All types of social interaction involve at least
some degree of trust. Think about all the people or things you trust
in the course of a typical day, in many cases, without giving it any
conscious thought. It makes you realize how many things in our lives
would come to a grinding halt if there was no trust.

There are times when we have to use common sense and not trust.
If a stranger drives up to you while you're walking along the sidewalk
and asks you to get in the car for a ride to wherever you are going,
it's probably a good idea to suspect something and politely decline.
Or, if you get an email from someone promising you large sums of
money in exchange for a small upfront fee or for your bank details,
it's best to not trust the sender and delete the message.

Part of my job includes writing about cybersecurity, and one of the
more popular topics in recent years is something called "zero trust."
This is a cybersecurity strategy in which no user or device is automatically trusted, regardless of whether they are inside or outside an
organization's network perimeter. It requires strict identity verifica-
tion and authorization for every access attempt, basically assuming
a breach could happen at any time and taking proactive measures
to defend against threats. A guiding principle of this is "never trust,
always verify."

It wouldn't make sense for us to adopt this approach in our personal lives. You wouldn't think of holding up a line at the grocery store
while you wait for a supervisor to come and verify that the cashier
is an actual employee of the store before handing over your money
to make a purchase. It does often come down to common sense and

life experiences. But for a good part of our existence, trust is essential. We can't live in a constant state of not trusting, or we'll become paranoid and not able to function.

I've had to undergo a number of surgeries over the years, and each time implicitly trusted that the surgeons and the medical staff knew what they were doing. I was going to be under anesthesia for a time and completely oblivious to what was going on. My life was literally in their hands. If I had not trusted these people, I would have declined the surgeries and put my life at risk. Even when we're worried or nervous about doing something, like having an operation, we're still able to summon the trust we need.

When I visited China years ago for a business trip, the authorities required me to turn over my passport for the duration of the trip. This was in the mid 1980s, when China was still a relatively closed country for foreign travel. There were only specific areas you were allowed to visit, and a heavy military presence made it a somewhat scary place to be. I was certainly nervous giving up my passport in this type of environment. But ultimately, I trusted that the government officials would return it, which they did just before I headed to the airport to catch my flight out of the country.

Being trustful among our families, friends, neighbors, coworkers, and others can lead to a number of benefits. In fact, trust is ultimately the foundation of any healthy relationship, whether it's with family members, friends, or people we hardly know or don't know at all.

One benefit of trust is reduced stress and anxiety. If you were riding in a bus across town and did not trust the bus driver, how relaxed do you think you would be? We need to be able to trust a lot of people in our lives for emotional and mental wellbeing.

Also, having a lot of people around you that you trust means you have a reliable network of family and friends who can help you and provide support during difficult times. You will likely have stronger and more stable relationships if you're around people you trust and who trust you. It would seem logical, then, that this would lead to increased happiness and satisfaction. And if you know you have a trusted support system to lean on during times of struggle and hardship, that can help you overcome challenges and bounce back from setbacks. If you've ever lost a job or had a serious health issue, you know how much it means to have people around you who you can trust.

Another possible benefit of trust is increased and improved communications. If you trust someone, you are more likely to communicate honestly with that person. Oftentimes, communication is vital for a healthy relationship. Any marriage or friendship that doesn't include healthy communication is not going to last. It's the people we trust who are likely to be there for us in good times and bad. That's why trust is so important. It's a foundational part of our interactions with others and strong relationships.

Most importantly, and often overlooked, is the ability to trust yourself. There is no one else in the world you have to deal with more than yourself. If you don't trust your own heart and mind, that can make for some stressful and fearful situations in life. It can be easy to lose trust in yourself. Maybe you've made a mistake at work and got called out by your boss. Or maybe someone has criticized you constantly. This can easily get you wondering about your ability to do things and make it harder to make decisions.

This has happened to me many times in my life. It's part of the experience. Many of us have messed up at work or been criticized or questioned about our decisions. It's perhaps at those times when we most need to come to our own aid and remind ourselves that we are trustworthy.

While there are dozens of examples of when I've had to trust my own decision-making ability and sanity, a few stand out in my mind as particularly memorable. One is when I was a teenager and playing ice hockey in a local league. We only had one goaltender on our team, and he got injured early in the season. The coach called the team together and asked if anyone wanted to volunteer to be the team's goalie.

I gave it a bit of thought, and then told the coach I would give it a try. Playing goalie in hockey is not always fun. In fact, it can be physically dangerous and emotionally nerve-racking. Besides having the opposing team—and your own during practice—shooting pucks at you, there's the pressure of being the last line of defense on the team.

It was a lot of work and not easy, and I was not a great goalie by any measure. But I'm glad I stepped forward. I trusted myself enough to bear the responsibilities and the risks. I gained a lot of respect from my teammates and coach. And perhaps more important, I learned a lot about myself.

Another decision, one that I mentioned earlier, was far more consequential for myself and my family. That was when I decided to become a freelance writer. I'd been laid off from my job on a technology publication, and was having no luck finding a new position. After giving it a lot of thought I decided to strike out on my own and create my own writing business. It was a risky move, but I trusted my work ethic and my ability to find clients. Trust of any kind can be a risk, and this certainly was. It turned out to be one of the best decisions I've ever made.

Finally, there was the decision to start a blog about positivity and gratitude. It was something I'd been thinking about for a while before I finally took the plunge. I had to trust that I'd be able to fit the extra work into my schedule, that I'd be able to devote the time necessary to turn out good posts and keep readers interested. I'm glad I did start it, because a lot of people have told me that the posts have inspired them in a number of ways. That was my goal, and the blog came about because I trusted myself to do what was needed to get it done.

An important part of trusting yourself is to *be* yourself, even as the world oftentimes calls you to be someone else. We all face situations or occasions where we feel a need to take on different personas, depending on who we are with or what's going on. It's almost like we become actors taking on roles, trying to be somebody else because, for whatever reason—insecurity or some other factor—we feel a need to do this.

For sure, there are times when this kind of behavior makes sense. You might take on a different persona or act differently when engaging with your boss or your grandmother than you would when spending time with your friends. At other times, it's just a bad habit that can have a negative impact on you and those around you.

I think so much of not being ourselves comes from worrying about other peoples' opinions of us, or comparing ourselves to others. It's one thing to admire someone's accomplishments. But it's another thing entirely to measure yourself against other people, only to identify your shortcomings and then feel badly about them. If you've found yourself trying to fit it in by changing who you really are and compromising your values and beliefs, or focusing too much on what other people think of you, or making unfair comparisons with others, maybe it's time for some self-appreciation.

A big part of self-trust is being comfortable with who you are, and recognizing your worth, strengths, and uniqueness. We each have something to contribute to the world, we each possess gifts to share, and we need to be grateful for who we are. Of course, this is not always easy. We are social creatures and, in some cases, we have to "be someone else" for one reason or another.

Every once in a while, I'll hear or read about people, perhaps celebrities or star athletes or just ordinary individuals, who people say acted the same no matter who they were with. These people are likely authentic, genuine, and sincere. And they probably trust themselves. It never ceases to make me stop and think about whether this is the way I am. We can all strive to be more genuine, and to treat ourselves with the love, respect, and trust we deserve.

There's a quote with uncertain origins that I think hits the mark: "What other people think of me is none of my business." The point is that we should not give other people the power to determine our self-worth or push us in certain directions based on their own opinions. We need self-confidence. Here are some ways I've learned to build trust in myself that might apply to you as well:

WHEN TAKING ON A TASK, SET REASONABLE GOALS FOR YOURSELF

Don't create scenarios where you make your objectives nearly impossible to meet, and then beat yourself up for failing. In a lot of cases, we aim too high with our goals. There is nothing wrong with being ambitious and setting lofty goals, but they need to be realistic. If they're not and you fail to reach them, the disappointment can be huge and you can lose trust in your ability to get things done.

Oftentimes when I take on a writing assignment, the client will suggest a deadline and ask me if it's reasonable. I carefully think through all that will be involved in completing the work before agreeing to the date, to ensure that I will be able to meet it and please the client. If I think I can get the work done even sooner, I'll give the client an even earlier date. If I think I'll need more time, I ask for it.

TREAT YOURSELF WITH COMPASSION

A lot of times we can be our own worst enemies and think negative thoughts about ourselves. We fall short and then start thinking negative thoughts and even call ourselves names.

But how can you trust yourself when you're in the midst of self-loathing? There's a common saying that you can't love others until you love yourself. It makes a lot of sense. You need to get rid of the negative thoughts about yourself and avoid self-criticism when you make mistakes. Everyone makes mistakes.

FOCUS ON YOUR STRENGTHS

I can confidently change a lightbulb and put together furniture that comes with clear instructions. But I will pass on installing a lighting fixture or putting a new roof on the house. I trust my ability to complete the former, but not the latter.

We are all better at some things and worse at others. That's just the way we're wired, with different skill sets. You hear about the Renaissance Man who is skilled at all of the tasks he takes on and has knowledge in many fields, but that's the exception. To build more trust in yourself, do more of the things you are good at, and maybe avoid the things you're not good at. You can always aim to learn new skills, but within your capabilities.

BE YOURSELF

This is perhaps most important of all. If you are afraid of how others will judge you, you might start acting like a different person than the individual you really are.

Trust who you are and your ability to make decisions and get things done. You are one of a kind in this world. No one else, out of all the billions of people on our planet, have had the same exact experiences you've had or share all of your capabilities. Whenever you begin feeling insecure around other people, remind yourself that it is okay to be yourself.

Whether it's trusting ourselves or trusting others, the importance of having trust can't be overstated. It's at the root of almost everything we do, whether we realize it or not. Trust me.

15

APPRECIATE
THE GIFT OF MUSIC

Some of my earliest memories are related to music. I remember, as a four-year-old, singing a song called "Daisy Bell (Bicycle Built for Two)," which I only recently discovered was written in 1892. Regardless of when it was written, my adoring parents were overjoyed by my rendition. I went on to sing in the glee club at my elementary and middle schools. And I also played the alto saxophone in the elementary school band. Unfortunately, none of these musical pursuits went beyond my early teenage years.

Still, music has been an important part of my life. Growing up in the 1960s, I listened to the Beatles, the Rolling Stones, the Monkees, and many other groups and singers on the radio, and then, in the 1970s, I started buying up vinyl records. Later, it was cassette tapes, then compact discs, and then Spotify. I've listened to many kinds of music over the years. I might not like all of it, but I try to appreciate the work that goes into making it. I've relied on music during some of my most difficult challenges, for entertainment, inspiration, or just distraction.

One of my prized possessions is a set of Apple headphones that I received as gift from Reneé a few years ago. I've relied on the headphones heavily during hospital stays, not only to enjoy the music but also to block out the nearly constant background noise. I gained a new appreciation for music during those long stays in the hospital. It provided a respite from the fear and uncertainty I was experiencing.

Music has always provided inspiration and fulfillment for people. In my blog, *Embracing Gratitude and Positivity,* I wrote about two women for whom music not only provides income and fulfillment, but a way to bring joy to others.

Donna Fields Brown is a retired registered nurse and professional musician who has had to overcome challenges including an abusive mother, severe asthma, and tinnitus. Growing up, Donna enjoyed listening to music on the radio, which inspired her to learn to play the guitar. After practicing for several years, she became proficient enough to join a rock band in the early 1970s called Medusa. The band played local gigs for three years until Donna left to go to nursing school, and Medusa split up shortly after. She gave up playing music to begin her career as a nurse, working at hospitals and senior care facilities for more than thirty years. After retiring she returned to playing live music.

Medusa's music had never received any recognition until 2012, when Donna received a phone call from a producer of a prominent Chicago record label, Numero Group, which asked for original tapes of the band's music. Within a year the group's album, *First Step Beyond*, was released to worldwide acclaim. A revamped version of the group, called Medusa1975, toured the country and received wild fanfare. The band was twice invited to play at SXSW Conference & Festivals in Austin, Texas.

Despite the ongoing battle with tinnitus—a condition in which a person perceives ringing or other noises in their ears—Donna continues to enjoy playing and listening to music. She, her husband Gary, and a third musician formed a trio and learned songs from the 1950s, 1960s, and 1970s. They play at several assisted living facilities, and the music brings great joy to the residents. Donna is enormously grateful for the chance to deliver this joy through music.

Natalia "Saw Lady" Paruz was a professional dancer, a trainee with the Martha Graham Dance Company of Contemporary Dance, a tap-dance teacher and demonstrator for Dance Masters and Dance Educators of America. She earned a living performing in musical theater. One day, on her way home from Lincoln Center in New York City, Natalia crossed a street and was hit by a speeding taxicab. She suffered permanent damage to her upper spine, which ended her dance career. Natalia was devastated, having dedicated her life to dance.

Sometime after while on a trip to Austria, Natalia attended a show and one of the acts was a musical saw player. She was mesmerized by the sound, which was different than anything she had heard before. When she got home, she purchased a handsaw from a hardware store, and a new career was born. Today, Natalia—the Saw Lady as she is professionally known—brings joy to countless people through her talent with the instrument. She has been a professional sawist for twenty-five years, and her music is on YouTube, Spotify, Amazon, as well as on all the major social media platforms. She has appeared at such venues as Carnegie Hall, Madison Square Garden, Lincoln Center—and the New York City subway system.

In fact, it's through her work in the subway system as a busker, or a street musician, that Natalia has enjoyed some of her most memorable and inspirational moments. Her favorite incident happened while she was playing at the Times Square station. A blind man joined a group of passers-by gathered around her, and his face lit up to the sound of the music. A lady from the crowd who had noticed the man's joy bought him one of Natalia's CDs and explained that it was the music he was hearing. Knowing that in a small way her music had been the impetus for such an act of kindness between two strangers was priceless to Natalia, and, all things considered, the awful car accident that ended her dance career turned out to be a blessing in disguise.

Music can have a powerful effect on us in many ways, including a number of health benefits. An article by Johns Hopkins Medicine, entitled, "Keep Your Brain Young with Music," notes that research has shown listening to music can decrease anxiety, blood pressure, and pain as well as enhance sleep quality, mood, mental alertness, and memory. Another article, posted on Healthline and entitled, "The Benefits of Listening to Music," notes that music has a way of uniting people and also offers individual benefits. "Music exerts a powerful influence on human beings," the article asserts. "It can boost memory, build task endurance, lighten your mood, reduce anxiety and depression, stave off fatigue, improve your response to pain, and help you work out more effectively."

To close out this chapter, I've put together a list of songs I've enjoyed over the years about positivity, gratitude, celebration, and hope, along with brief descriptions based on an amalgam of critiques and, in some cases, my own commentary. They run across a variety of genres and eras, and each is uplifting in its own way.

- **"All Star"** by Smash Mouth. This became a pop culture phenomenon, known for its catchy melody and upbeat tempo.

It was written in response to fan letters the band received from kids who felt like they were outsiders.

- **"As I Lay Me Down to Sleep"** by Sophie B. Hawkins. Despite having themes of longing and loss, this song carries a message of hope and optimism. It was popular at the time I received a kidney transplant from my wife Reneé, and gave me lots of comfort during a frightening time.

- **"Celebration"** by Kool and the Gang. It's no wonder this song is played at so many happy occasions. It's a song about joy, unity, festivity, and the spirit of celebration. The lyrics inspire people to come together, enjoy themselves, and embrace the moment.

- **"Counting Stars"** by OneRepublic. This song suggests that people should focus on their dreams and aspirations rather than on financial security and material possessions. It emphasizes pursuing a life filled with purpose and meaning.

- **"Don't Stop"** by Fleetwood Mac. When I was in college this was one of the big hits off the *Rumors* album. It encourages perseverance, reminding us to keep moving toward our goals even when faced with challenges or setbacks.

- **"Don't Stop Believin'"** by Journey. Another song that focuses on perseverance, hope, and resilience, encouraging listeners to keep trying even when facing adversity.

- **"Don't Worry, Be Happy"** by Bobby McFerrin. This song encourages a positive outlook, emphasizing that we have the power to choose how we react to life's challenges. It encourages us to enjoy the present moment rather than dwelling on worries.

- **"Eye of the Tiger"** by Survivor. This is an inspirational song from one of the *Rocky* movies, about resilience, determination, overcoming challenges, and keeping dreams of the past alive.

- **"Gratitude"** by Earth, Wind & Fire. Gratitude is so important in life, and this uplifting song makes that clear. It celebrates the joy of music and the power of positive emotions.

- **"Happy"** by Pharrell Williams. As the title suggests, this upbeat song is all about the pursuit of joy. It encourages listeners to embrace happiness and look for reasons to be happy, even in times of struggle.

- **"Here Comes the Sun"** by The Beatles. Some music critics and fans consider this to be one of the group's best songs. It's easy to see why. Not only is it a beautiful song, but it's upbeat and has a message of finding hope and a fresh start after a difficult period.

- **"How Great Thou Art"** by Carl Boberg. This song encourages listeners to reflect on God's greatness and wonder. Carrie Underwood's rendition of it along with Vince Gill is a powerful, inspiring performance of a hymn that celebrates the awe-inspiring nature of God.

- **"I Can See Clearly Now"** by Johnny Nash. This is a song about overcoming adversity and discovering hope in the face of difficulties. It reminds us that if you're going through a rough time, brighter days are ahead.

- **"I Gotta Feeling"** by the Black Eyed Peas. Sometimes we just have to let loose and find happiness in the moment, especially during difficult times. That's what this song is about.

- **"I'm a Believer"** by the Monkees. I remember watching the Monkees' television show, which was innovative and ahead of its time in the use of music videos. This song is about hope and finding joy, even after facing disappointment. Embrace optimism and believe.

- **"Joy to the World"** by Three Dog Night. A nice, uplifting message of peace, joy, hope, and unity, which was really needed in the world when the song was released, as it still is today.

- **"Just the Way You Are"** by Billy Joel. I went to a Billy Joel concert in college and then another forty-two years later, and he put on a great show at each. This song is about recognizing and celebrating someone's innate beauty.

- **"Mr. Blue Sky"** by Electric Light Orchestra. ELO is one of my favorites and I really enjoy listening to this song. It has an uplifting melody and lyrics and calls to mind a sense of hope and optimism, even in the face of difficult times. It has become a feel-good anthem.

- **"Music Box Dancer"** by Frank Mills. During a hospital stay following a serious health scare, this song popped into my head. I'm not sure why it did, but this uplifting, cheerful instrumental piece helped me through a difficult time.

- **"Ode to Joy"** (from Symphony No. 9) by Ludwig van Beethoven. This is a powerful expression of joy and the triumph of the human spirit. It has become a symbol of unity and hope, something we desperately need in the world today.

- **"Put a Little Love in Your Heart"** by Jackie DeShannon. The lyrics, "put a little love in your heart… and the world will be a better place," say it all. The song encourages kindness, empathy, and unity. Again, the world could use a lot more of this.

- **"Somewhere Over the Rainbow"** by Israel (IZ) Kamakawiwo'Ole. Like millions of others, I first heard this sung by Judy Garland in *The Wizard of Oz*. But the version by IZ is beautiful and inspiring in its own way. I recall walking down the main street of Waikiki in Hawaii and hearing it playing constantly—and never getting tired of it.

- **"Thank You for Being a Friend"** by Andrew Gold. Good friends are there for us in good times and bad. This song is about the significant impact friends can have on our lives, and expresses gratitude for the gift of friendship.

- **"Thank You for Loving Me"** by Bon Jovi. This song celebrates the power of love and emotional support. It expresses profound gratitude for a partner's steadfast love and support in the midst of challenges.

- **"Three Little Birds"** by Bob Marley. This song has a simple, positive message about why we need to stop worrying, and encourages us to embrace optimism and find peace amid the difficulties of life.

- **"We Are Family"** by Sister Sledge. It's hard not to be inspired by this uplifting song, which promotes the importance of family, unity, and the need to embrace community and support each other.

- **"What a Wonderful World"** by Louis Armstrong. I find it hard not to get emotional when listening to this song. It's about appreciating the simple joy and beauty of the world, like the colors of a rainbow, and offers a message of hope and positivity.

.

16

TRY PATIENCE

When I was a teenager, I worked part-time in a bowling alley to earn some spending money. One of my many responsibilities was to retrieve bowling balls when they would get stuck in the automatic ball return system. Normally, after a ball knocked down pins it would fall into a ball pit, then a conveyor belt would move it up a ramp, returning it to the player, using gravity through a track system under the alley. When a ball got stuck, I would have to open trap doors over the ball return ramp to find and grab the ball and return it to the bowler. This would usually happen when young children rolled the balls down the lanes very slowly. And it happened a lot.

If the bowling alley was crowded and I was particularly busy, having to retrieve stuck balls sometimes tried my patience. It wasn't the bowlers that were annoying—these were just youngsters with their parents enjoying a fun outing at the lanes—it was the system and its flaws that made me sometimes feel like I could be making better use of my time.

A lot of us struggle with impatience. I know I do. The ability to accept or tolerate delays, problems, or suffering without getting annoyed or stressed out—the definition of patience—is just not easy.

Recently, my wife and I took a trip to California to visit our older son and daughter-in-law. The upshot is we had a wonderful time, enjoying the sights, the pleasant weather, the food, and most of all the company. What wasn't so much fun was having our patience tested a few times at the start of the trip. We left our house for JFK International Airport about three hours before the scheduled departure, even though we live about thirty-five minutes away. Anyone who lives in metro areas like New York or Los Angeles knows that you really need to build in lots of extra time to get to the airport. Well, in this case, it wasn't enough time. It was a rainy morning, the traffic was awful, and it took us far longer than it should have to arrive at the airport.

When we reached the security checkpoint at the Delta Airlines terminal, I told the TSA agent that I had a prosthetic left leg. The agent said I should go through the metal detector and speak with another agent on the other side. The other agent asked me to sit down while he scanned the prosthetic with an explosives trace detector, and then instructed me to see yet another agent to receive a full-body pat down. In the midst of this I received an alert on my Apple Watch telling me that our plane was boarding. Not surprisingly, the TSA agent was unimpressed by the alert and ignored my concerns about missing the plane.

When I finally got through security and after we gathered up our belongings, we headed to our gate. Now, JFK has some big terminals and we happened to be in the largest one, and our gate was the farthest away from where we were. We had to hustle and barely made it to the plane on time.

I know this is a story that most air travelers can relate to—well, maybe not the prosthetic part. And yes, in retrospect we probably should have left home for the airport earlier than we did. And believe me, I understand the need for security at the airport. I just wanted to illustrate how life can throw frustrating, time-consuming situations at us that can dampen our moods in a hurry. I didn't complain much out loud, but was not pleased about sitting in bumper-to-bumper traffic or needing to practically run to catch a plane on one real leg.

I must admit that a lot of negative thoughts passed through my mind as we made our way from home to the plane: Why do we live in a place where bumper-to-bumper traffic is practically a given? Why is TSA treating me like a genuine security risk when the last time I traveled I breezed through the process? Why does it feel like we're walking to Los Angeles on the way to the gate? Why didn't I think to bring that bag of Chex Mix from home rather than overpaying for snacks on the plane?

Sometimes, and under certain situations, it can be super difficult to be patient. But that's when we most need to put things into context to help us deal with the situation. In this instance, the worst-case scenario was we would miss the plane and have to catch a later one—a relatively mild inconvenience, all things considered. The trick in staying patient was to remind myself that this was not a catastrophic situation. Although the trip might have started out annoying, the positive reason for the trip—going to visit our son and daughter-in-law—helped to outweigh the short-term aggravation. In this case, keeping things in perspective helped to alleviate the stress.

Patience goes hand in hand with qualities such as perseverance and dedication. It's patience that enables you to accept delays, perseverance that keeps you going despite difficulties, and dedication that keeps you committed to a goal or task even when it's challenging.

A little curiosity and research led me to some fascinating stories of people who exhibited patience in wildly different ways.

Michaelangelo—whose full name, Michelangelo di Lodovico Buonarroti Simoni, might take some patience to write if you had to do it a lot—was an Italian sculptor, painter, architect, poet, and engineer of the High Renaissance period. He is credited with the quote, "Genius is eternal patience," which summarizes the belief that true genius isn't just about innate talent, but also about enduring the long and demanding process of creation.

Michaelangelo would know. Over a four-year period, he painted the ceiling of the Sistine Chapel in Vatican City. During this project, he had to deal with the physical strain of painting sixty feet in the air on a curved surface in awkward positions, including lying on his back on wooden scaffolding. He did this with the added pressures of time constraints and high expectations.

Nelson Mandela, the South African leader who was imprisoned for twenty-seven years for opposing apartheid, the system of legalized racial segregation that was in place in his country, chose to be patient rather than bitter and angry over this ordeal, so he could focus on long-term goals and take action at the right moment in time. Mandela used his time in prison to prepare for the moment when he could make a difference, including helping to negotiate an end to apartheid and becoming the first democratically elected president of South Africa.

Another person who exhibited extraordinary patience was Katherine Johnson, an African American mathematician at NASA whose work was critical to the space agency's success in putting an American in orbit and landing others on the moon. Johnson's mathematical calculations for the Mercury and Apollo space missions required enormous patience, as she faced discrimination and segregation for being a Black woman in an environment dominated by white men.

Her efforts, chronicled in the movie, *Hidden Figures*, earned her the Presidential Medal of Freedom in 2015.

Finally, there is Charles Darwin, who spent more than twenty years developing and refining his ideas such as the theory of evolution by natural selection. He conducted meticulous research, including observations and data collection in the field, and long periods of reflection, before coming to his conclusions about complex scientific problems. Darwin was quoted as saying that one of the most important qualities leading to his success as a man of science was "unbounded patience in long reflecting over any subject."

These people, and so many more throughout history, remind us that with patience we can accomplish a lot. You don't have to paint a masterpiece, change history, help get people into space, or develop ground-breaking scientific theories. You can set and meet your own goals.

Many situations in life can become tests of our patience. Here are some examples of common ones that resonate with me and might help you put patience into practice:

- **Mastering new skills.** Becoming skilled at something new, such as learning a second language or how to play a musical instrument, requires lots of patience and persistence. As you're working through your lessons, think of how satisfying it will be when you feel confident enough to demonstrate the new skill. Like, being able to play the piano at family events, or traveling to another country and understanding the language.

- **Improving yourself.** Attempts at self-improvement, such as breaking bad habits, can take a long time. But just the fact that you are working toward a goal, even when the progress is slow, can be rewarding. Like mastering new skills, focus on the ultimate outcome of your efforts.

- **Trying to lose weight.** Along the same lines, dieting requires lots of patience. Depending on how much weight you're trying to lose, you're not likely to meet your goal overnight. This is a case of developing self-control, sometimes for a matter of weeks or months, before you begin to see results. Rejoice when you get on the scale and see that your weight has gone down, and think of the pleasure of being able to fit into a new dress or suit.

- **Trying to gain weight.** I have to include this because you wouldn't ordinarily think of this as requiring patience. But I've been in situations following serious health issues where I've lost a lot of weight. Gaining it back while at the same time sticking to a healthy diet is not as easy as you think. While doing this I tried to think of how lucky I was to be on the other side of the diet equation.

- **Waiting in line.** No matter where this occurs—at a bank, in the grocery store, at the post office, at an amusement park, at a ballpark food vendor—it's easy to lose patience if the line seems to be moving too slowly. Remember, everyone else in the line is also trying to be patient. Try to remember how fortunate it is that you are able to be out and about accomplishing something, even as simple as mailing a letter.

- **Waiting for an appointment.** I've had to sit in a lot of doctors' waiting rooms over the last few years, sometimes for inordinately long periods of time. I always try to remember to bring a book, crossword puzzle, or something else to keep me occupied. Doing something while you're waiting, no matter how mundane, can help pass the time.

- **Sitting in a traffic jam.** As I noted in my own example above, traffic can be a major factor in our lives because we spend so much of our time going from place to place. Drivers especially need to exercise patience when in the midst of traffic jams or slowdowns, but so do passengers. Listening to music or audiobooks, playing travel games, or just having nice conversation can help make the waiting more tolerable.

- **Saving up to buy something.** A lot of times in our lives we'd like to have something but need to come up with the money to pay for it. Depending on what it is we want to buy, this could take days, weeks, months, and even years. But saving up for something fun can be satisfying in its own right. When I was a kid, I used to save up money from allowances and doing chores to buy Matchbox cars for about fifty cents apiece. It's hard to imagine that seeming like a lot of money, but it did.

- **Waiting for a garden to grow.** Anyone who has planted vegetables or flowers knows you need patience to grow a garden. It oftentimes starts with a little seed and eventually becomes a plant that delivers the goods. As you're watering and otherwise caring for your garden, think about the miracle of a tiny seed becoming a plant that will reward you for your patience.

Think of patience-testing incidents from your own life over the last few days. Did you need more patience dealing with your commute, your boss, your coworkers, your clients, your spouse, your kids, your nosy neighbors? Ordinary life situations constantly put us in the position of needing patience, whether we like it or not. How well we react to frustrating or stressful situations can depend on a lot of things, including our mood, health, quality of sleep, etc. What tests our patience one day might not even be on the radar screen the next. If we're aware ahead of time of what triggers our impatience—say, a failure to put things into context—we can take proactive steps to avoid feeling impatient about things.

When we're not feeling one hundred percent, sometimes even relatively minor incidents can set us off in the wrong direction and cause us to lose patience. Some time ago, I was at my cardiologist's office for a follow-up visit after my cardiac arrest, and he told me he had to change out one of my medications because it was affecting my kidney. It made sense from a medical standpoint, but for some reason this change pushed me over the edge and I got angry—not at the doctor but at the situation. I had been through a lot with my health, and this incident reminded me that I was not as healthy as I wanted to be.

To change my mood and patiently accept the change, I decided to focus on the positives. These drugs that I take enable me to have a working, transplanted kidney and are regulating my heart function. They provide me with the ability to enjoy day-to-day activities. When I looked at it from that standpoint, changed medicines was not a big deal.

The Cleveland Clinic, in a June 2024 article entitled, "How to Be Patient: 6 Strategies to Help You Keep Your Cool," notes that patience is a skill that everyone can develop and strengthen, and offers a few tips for helping with patience when life is difficult or when things aren't moving fast enough.

One is to practice mindfulness, which will help you appreciate the present moment, without judging. It will help you pay attention to what you are doing, how you are feeling, and what is going on around you. When you're standing in a slow-moving line, it's easy to begin thinking about all kinds of things that will just get you aggravated: the chores you need to do at home, the work project that's running late, the rising price of groceries. Practicing mindfulness, through breathing techniques, can help calm your mind and make the wait easier.

Another tip is to know what you can control. Are you able to change your circumstances, or not? You can't control the flow of traffic on your way to work. But you are able to check GPS for a better route. Consider the popular "Serenity Prayer" for guidance: "God, grant me the serenity to accept the things I cannot change, the courage to change the things I can, and the wisdom to know the difference."

It's also a good idea to keep things lighthearted and try to find the funny aspects of a situation when you're starting to lose your patience. Laughing, even smiling, can help to lighten the mood.

Finally, practice empathy. It's always dangerous to assume things about people without knowing what they are going through. If you're getting impatient about a lack of response to your emails to someone and assume they are ignoring you, consider instead that the individual might be in the midst of a crisis and unable to respond.

Becoming more patient is a lifelong undertaking. We all struggle with this, and it's virtually impossible to completely master this virtue. All we can do is try to get better at being patient.

On the plus side, taking the patient route can pay dividends. Years ago, I was in a frustrating job at a company with a tyrannical owner who created nearly constant stress. After one particularly traumatic day, I decided I was going to quit. I told my dad about my plans and he advised me to be patient, to stick with the job until something better came along. He knew it would be easier for me to find a new job if I was currently employed.

I took the advice and, sure enough, a better job and employer that would change the course of my life was just around the corner. In imparting his wisdom, my father used three words I have never forgotten: *bide your time*. This is the essence of patience, a virtue that's difficult to master but beautiful to embrace.

17

RESILIENCE— YOU GOT THIS!

Everyone endures hardship and shows resilience to some extent. I've been challenged in this area in ways I never imagined possible. Nor could I have imagined how crucial resilience—the ability to adapt to stressful or traumatic events, maintaining psychological wellbeing in the face of hardship or adversity—has been to my survival.

While some people might have a greater ability to bounce back from difficulties than others, everyone has an innate capacity for being resilient. And we can all learn to be more resilient through our experiences and the need to develop coping mechanisms. Being resilient doesn't mean you won't be hurt or disappointed by things. It also doesn't mean you won't or can't have negative emotional reactions, even depression, during or following difficult events. It *does* mean you will not remain in that dark place.

I had to call on resilience a few years ago, with a big assist from my family, when I faced a major health problem. The way I look at it there really wasn't much of a choice: be resilient or fall into a downward spiral of misery and despair. There was no middle ground. As I've mentioned, in March 2023 I went to the hospital because my left foot was bothering me a lot. I ended up having it amputated because of vascular disease. While that in itself was a challenge, within a matter of days things got even worse.

Initially, I was doing fairly well following the surgery. In fact, the morning after the operation, a physical therapist came to see me in the hospital and encouraged me to get out of bed that morning and try to walk a bit with a walker. Using the walker, I hopped down the hallway and back to my room. The therapist was pleased and enthusiastic about how well I did. I looked forward to the next session as I worked my way toward getting a prosthetic leg.

Soon after, a case worker signed me up for a rehabilitation program that was to take place at another facility beginning in a few days. My abilities to bounce back were in full force and I even made plans to squeeze in some work time between exercise sessions at the rehab facility. In the meantime, my sons Andrew and Tim, who live in the Los Angeles and Boston areas, respectively, who had been visiting, went back to their homes thinking I was on the mend.

Unfortunately, a few days later my health began to decline in a hurry. One morning I woke up feeling extremely weak and thought I was dehydrated. My breathing became increasingly difficult and my blood pressure began to drop—apparently, my body was not getting enough oxygen. Before long I went into respiratory failure, then congestive heart failure, and my kidney function began to decline.

The doctors overseeing my case moved me to the surgical intensive care unit (ICU) in critical condition. The medical staff gave me a respiratory device to help with breathing, and the continuous influx of oxygen made it difficult to speak. I was becoming acutely aware of the fact that I was dying. I could feel it. Soon it became clear to the doctors that this had gone beyond surgical complications. It had become more of a heart issue, and I was quickly moved into the cardiac ICU. Each move involved multiple staff members and devices to ensure my safety during the transfer.

My wife called my sons to let them know how bad things had gotten, and they both hopped on planes and came back to New York. At one point, the resident cardiologist in the ICU and his team came into my room to discuss the possible diagnostic and treatment options. All of them sounded frightening and unappealing, especially the option of open-heart surgery.

The first procedure they would perform would be something called a transesophageal echocardiography (TEE), a test that takes pictures of your heart using high-frequency sound waves. This test would give the doctors more detailed information, so they could have a better idea of how to proceed. To do the test, and to enable my organs to get the oxygen they so desperately needed, I would need to be put on a ventilator for an indefinite period. Even in my semi-conscious state, I was adamant about not wanting to be on the ventilator for a prolonged period of time. Reneé understood my wishes on this.

With my body failing and my spirits declining by the minute, I was leaning toward not going ahead with any more procedures. I felt as if I was finished battling. My energy was gone, my resilience depleted. It was then that Reneé, Andrew, and Tim all said they thought it was worth at least doing the test to get a better idea of what condition my heart was in, and then see what the options were. They were not ready to give up and lose me.

I remember struggling with my feelings, not wanting to fight what seemed like an unwinnable fight at that point. I'm sure the sedative drugs they had me on didn't help in terms of letting me think straight. After a while, I came to the conclusion that they were right. As much as I did not want to face additional and potentially risky procedures, I could not let my family down. I couldn't give up on my life without at least giving this a chance and fighting on a bit longer, although I realized at that point the odds were against me.

As we waited for the medical team to put me on the respirator, I could not speak easily because of the breathing device they had me on. All I could do was mumble a few words. At that point, I realized my time might be short so I began writing goodbye messages to my family; it just felt like something I needed to do. It was heartbreaking, but I forged ahead with what I thought might be the last writing I would ever do.

I scribbled on notebook pages as best I could, blinking tears away. I felt a sense of urgency to complete the letters before the medical staff arrived, as though it were a final deadline after decades of facing deadlines on assignments in my career as a writer. My hope was that my letters, what I thought would be my last words to them, would be something that they could hold onto after I was gone. In return, my sons wrote me letters; not letters of goodbye but of gratitude and encouragement. It was a beautiful expression of love between us. I treasured the words they wrote to me that day and will continue to treasure them. This was truly a special moment in the midst of a very traumatic, frightening time.

While we continued to wait for the test to begin, a Catholic priest came into my room to lead us in a few prayers. This was very comforting and provided me with a sense of hope and peace. When the medical staff arrived to do the procedure, I waved goodbye to my loved ones. Although I felt sad, I wasn't really afraid. After being given another sedative, I drifted off to sleep, saying a silent prayer.

I'm not sure how long I was out but, as I slowly began to regain consciousness, I opened my eyes and saw a sign on the wall that said something like, "Welcome to the Cardiac ICU" and I was happy to have made it through the procedure. Because I was still on the respirator and heavily medicated, I experienced a surreal feeling of being alive and yet not alive at the same time. It felt as if I was existing in a strange place between life and death. I struggled to come to grips with exactly what was going on. One thing I immediately realized was that I was still on the ventilator. It was uncomfortable, and I kept drooling down my neck. I couldn't relax. How long will I need to be on this, I wondered. To communicate with my family and the staff, I continued to scribble messages on notebook pages. The hours drifted by slowly. Still sedated, I drifted in and out of sleep.

Then, a remarkable thing happened. My body began to recover. The doctors were amazed as the condition of my heart and lungs improved dramatically over the next few hours. My kidney took a bit longer to rebound and there had been some talk of putting me on dialysis. Fortunately, the kidney doctors following my case were positive that my kidney would also make a full recovery, and dismissed the idea of any immediate intervention.

Within a day I was taken of the ventilator and able to breathe on my own. This made me feel so much more comfortable, and provided evidence that I was going in the right direction. Soon after, I was moved out of the ICU to a regular cardiac floor. I remained there for a week and a half before moving on to the rehab facility, where I learned how I would manage to live with one foot.

There is much to take away from this experience in terms of

resilience. It starts with my family, because without them it would have been difficult to find the strength and determination to survive. I was nearly ready to give up, but it wasn't my time and I needed to be reminded of that. It meant so much to me to have family members there for support. Sometimes it's the most challenging experiences that enable us to realize how much we are loved and how much we appreciate those around us for giving us reasons to be resilient.

This episode marked the second time within less than a year that I nearly lost my life due to a serious illness or incident. It goes without saying that it was traumatizing, frightening, and humbling. It also made me realize how important resilience is not only for survival, but for living a life that's fulfilling. If you don't embrace resilience, the meaning and beauty and preciousness of life can begin to slip away in a hurry. There's no point of living life with a defeatist attitude. Even in the darkest times, there is light. We just have to give ourselves a chance to see it, sometimes through sheer willpower. As Mahatma Gandhi said, "Strength does not come from physical capacity. It comes from an indomitable will."

The two near-death experiences have given me reasons for deep soul-searching. But one thing is clear to me: those of us who have been given extra chances in life have every reason to be grateful for each day and for the resilience that keeps us around. Perhaps even more important, we have been given the opportunity—maybe even the obligation—to serve as inspirations for those around us. So, in effect, resilience comes with responsibility.

I needed additional resilience in the coming months as I learned how to walk with a prosthetic leg. The first model I received was heavy, awkward, and required that I wear about a dozen socks to keep the device from wobbling around as I walked. It was overwhelming trying to get used to the idea of putting it on and trying to keep my balance. I knew from research that not everyone is able to wear these devices and I was not sure it would work for me. But I made up my mind to try and to keep trying, because it was the only option I had for walking on my own.

For someone accustomed to walking seven or eight miles a day, it required a lot of willpower for me just to take a few steps. But I was determined to master walking with the prosthetic. I wanted to be somewhat independent again rather than depending on others for so many things. Within a year, and with a new and lighter prosthetic, I was able to walk much longer distances. I made it a goal to walk about three miles a day and, so far, I've been able to achieve that. Each step is a triumph, thanks to the prosthetic, my body's ability to recover, and my resilience.

I'm not the only one who's been tested in the resilience department. Over my lifetime, I've had the good fortune to witness a lot of people who have shown me the meaning of human strength and courage. They each provided lessons for how to bounce back from adversity and make the most of opportunities.

One was a man who was using the same physical therapy facility as I was when I was trying to regain strength and learn how to use the prosthetic. He was missing both of his feet as well as both hands. I was in awe and near disbelief as I watched him put on his prosthetic legs using his prosthetic hands. He had become so adept at doing this that it seemed to come naturally to him. At one point, he was vigorously running on a treadmill, supported by tethers to keep him from falling off. Watching him provided me with a valuable lesson in grit and resilience, at a time when I was struggling to embrace a new normal. Most striking to me was his attitude; upbeat and engaging, full of enthusiasm, positivity, and purpose. Seeing him reinforced my thinking that losing a limb was not a reason to be morose, or to give up on enjoying a good quality of life.

Another story of resilience comes from a man I've never met but had the privilege of profiling in my blog. Samuel Jimenez Coreas is from El Salvador, and his story is chronicled in a book called *Do Not Discard* by Marlene Byrne. Sam was born with a skin infection, and his parents couldn't afford medical care so they tried to sell him, without success, and ended up throwing him in the trash. Fortunately, a local baker spotted Sam at the trash dump, pulled him out, and took care of him. Four years later, Sam and the baker were delivering bread in the community when a group of gang members shot both of them. The baker drove them to the hospital, where he died. The bullet that hit Sam had grazed the back of his skull.

After that incident, authorities placed Sam in a government operated orphanage in San Salvador, from which he fled and lived on the streets for about two years. Just surviving was a challenge, and Sam and his friends had to steal food, clothes, and medicine to stay alive. He ended up back at the orphanage, which sent him to Nuestros Pequeños Hermanos, an orphanage in El Salvador that changed Sam's life forever by providing him with unconditional love, an education, a home, healthcare, and other opportunities that he had never experienced before.

Sam went on to attend college in Chicago, launch a career, and start a family. He has managed to remain resilient and positive in the face of so much adversity by embracing the challenges. "They are part of my life," Sam says. "Regardless of your past, there is no 'poor me' in this world." That attitude has helped him to maintain balance in his life. From such tragic and humble beginnings, he has made a happy and successful life for himself. It's a story of courage, resilience, and striving to realize dreams and achieve goals.

We all have our own challenges to face, whether they be physical, emotional, psychological, social, or some combination of all these. The trick is to not give up, despite the hurdles. My childhood friend, Steven Work, with whom I used to play street hockey, likes to tell me to keep shooting the puck at the net. It's his way of saying *keep persevering*.

We have all been given the gift of life, and along with it come the struggles that are part of the human experience. We've also all received built-in resiliency. At times it's difficult to reach down deep and tell yourself you are capable of taking the first steps. But if you can do that, the rest often just falls into place and you begin to regain your sense of purpose, joy, and wonder.

18

SET GOALS EVERY DAY

My family has a tradition where, at the end of each year, we individually list our highlights from the previous year and our goals for the next one. Then we compare notes, reminisce a bit about experiences we've shared over the past twelve months, and look ahead to what we hope to accomplish in the future. I have found it's good to have something to aim for in a new year. When we think about things we want to accomplish, we give ourselves a start at actually achieving them.

One of the biggest mistakes people make when they set goals is making them too generic and without any kind of timeframe. Someone might say, "My goal is to lose weight," or "My goal is to lose ten pounds in the first three months of the year." The latter is more specific than the former, and provides something tangible to aim for, whereas the former is too vague. I try to be specific whenever I create goals. For instance, I set a goal of walking an average of three miles a day for the entire year. By being specific with the goal, I can check my iPhone to see if I'm meeting my objective.

It's also important to be realistic about goals. Saying your goal is to launch into space on a rocket and orbit the Earth without any preparation is probably a bit over the top, although interesting. Another good practice is to have an accountability partner, someone who can check on your progress and maybe provide some encouragement now and then. Writing down your progress can also help because you can easily see how you're doing with meeting your goals.

A lot of us associate goals with longer-term objectives, giving ourselves weeks, months, or even years to accomplish something. Setting longer-term goals is great, but so is setting daily goals. Many of us are already doing this, we just haven't formalized it.

In the months following major thoracic surgery in the fall of 2025, I had a difficult time moving in certain ways. But during that time, I gave myself a daily goal of making my bed. At first, it was a real challenge. As I recuperated it became easier, but even so each time I accomplished this task I made a mental note that I had achieved that goal. To a lot of people who make their beds without giving it a thought, this might sound like a ridiculously low bar to set. Making a bed is second nature, just one of a long list of daily tasks. But when even something this simple becomes more difficult than it used to be, accomplishing it can be much more satisfying than it used to be.

Every day I try to set doable objectives for myself that I can aim to achieve within a day. Accomplishing things we set out to do, no matter how small and simple they might be, can make us feel good. It brings a bit of positivity into our lives, and we can all use more of that. And setting goals is something we can do at every stage of our lives.

Setting daily goals can deliver a lot of benefits. For one thing, it can keep us more motivated to do what's important in our lives. If it's imperative that you tend to your garden each day, then making that a goal can help ensure that the garden receives the attention you want it to have.

Daily goals can help us to be more productive by breaking down larger goals into smaller, daily tasks. I do this a lot with assignments. I'll set a goal to finish a portion of an assignment on that day. I do this for a week and I've completed the assignment and it's ready to go to the client.

Another benefit is reducing procrastination. If you set daily goals, it's harder to keep putting things off that you need to get done. Let's say you've been delaying making that dentist appointment because you don't want to go to the dentist. If you set a goal of calling to make the appointment by 2 p.m. on a particular day, maybe you're less likely to keep stalling on something you know you should do.

Daily goals can also help with time management, something many of us struggle with. You can prioritize your tasks and give yourself enough time to complete them. I used to do this all the time when I was juggling a dozen or so assignments at one time. I'd rank them by importance and focus on the ones with the tightest deadlines, then aim to get a given amount of work done on the highest-ranked assignments.

Along the lines of less procrastination and better time management, by setting daily goals we can enhance our self-discipline. Sometimes it's hard to stay focused on what we need to do. If you set it in your mind that you will achieve things on a certain day, you will be your own accountability partner. Finally, as I mentioned earlier, setting daily goals can give us a sense of accomplishment and satisfaction that makes us feel better about ourselves. Think about how rewarding it is whenever you cross items off of a to-do list. Why not do this each day?

Some goals can actually take up much of our day. After I was laid off from my job in the early 1990s, I decided to break up the days into thirds and aim to achieve something in each of those thirds. The first portion was devoted to job searching. I'd scour the Internet and when I'd find good fits I'd send in my resume, applying for a certain number of jobs each day. The second portion was dedicated to finding and working on freelance assignments, setting goals such as completing one quarter of an assignment that day, or sending out a hundred emails to prospective clients. And the third portion was spent working on my first book, *New Life*. I would set a goal to write a certain number of words or pages that day, or complete one interview as part of my research.

In my experience, one of the best times to set goals is when you're recovering from a setback and need encouragement. After I was fitted with a prosthetic left foot following my amputation, I had to learn how to walk with it. This was unlike anything I had ever done before.

Just learning how to wear the device was a challenge. I had to first place a silicone liner with a metal pin attachment at the end over my residual leg, by rolling it on. Then I had to put on the appropriate number of socks over the liner to ensure a tight fit with the socket. Next, I would ensure the pin on the bottom of the liner was in line with an opening in the socket and insert my leg into the prosthetic socket, which was attached to an artificial foot. I would listen for a certain number of clicks to ensure that the socket was securely attached.

At first, I would wear the prosthetic for a specific amount of time each day, gradually increasing the amount of time as the weeks went on. Once I was comfortable enough to walk without a walker, I began to set daily goals for steps. For someone accustomed to walking seven or eight miles a day, it was a humbling experience aiming to walk a fraction of that distance. But it was a start, and I gradually walked longer distances as time went on, setting new goals whenever

I felt I had mastered a certain distance. In time, I became adept at putting on the prosthetic, to the point where I hardly think about it during the process. Walking with the prosthetic has also become second nature. It's how I get around. I'm grateful for the opportunity to be mobile on my own, and setting daily goals is helping to strengthen my legs.

I've put together a list of things that might trigger ideas for possible daily goals. Some of these are "starters" to help jump-start you on long-term projects. Perhaps this list can help inspire you!

- **Call someone you haven't spoken to in a while**. Cold-calling someone can be awkward, but I have to think in the majority of cases people appreciate it. They can always not answer. It's especially gratifying to call someone who lives alone and maybe doesn't hear from a lot of people. You might make someone's day by just spending a few moments on a call.

- **Write a letter**. People used to send handwritten letters all the time. My mother once handed me a bunch of envelopes filled with letters I had written home when I was in college. I couldn't believe how many letters there were— or how good my penmanship was in those days! Imagine how surprised, and grateful, someone would be to receive a handwritten letter.

- **Volunteer somewhere**. This can be at a library, a soup kitchen, a nursing home, an animal shelter, or whatever makes sense for you. The point is to start the journey by making a call, sending an email or going in person. Seeing the gratitude on someone's face when you've done something nice or knowing you made a difference is great. But even beside that, it's a good use of your time on Earth.

- **Take some photos.** Set a time to take pictures with your phone or camera. You might take some that you end up sharing on Instagram, or maybe just with your family, or enjoying by yourself. There are artificial intelligence applications that let you turn your photo subjects into Pixar characters or Renaissance period landscapes.

- **Start writing a book, a blog, or a play.** I did this. Well, not the play. It took a long time to start, years actually, but once I did, I was on a roll and began to set daily goals for getting posts or chapters done. Incidentally, someone suggested I consider writing a play. It's outside my realm of expertise. But who knows, maybe someday.

- **Go walking or hiking.** If you set a time to hit the trail you might be more inclined to actually do it. Despite the health issues I've had to deal with, I still try to meet daily step goals. When the weather is nice, walking outside can make for a great break from work.

- **Try a new recipe.** I'm not a cook, except for barbecuing in the summer. But I've watched a lot of cooking shows and I enjoy trying new things now and then. If you like to prepare meals or bake, why not try something new?

- **Go kite flying with your kids.** Or take them to a local park or to the seashore or wherever. Time passes quickly, and quality time spent with your children is precious. I'm forever grateful for the times I've gotten to do that.

- **Start learning a new skill or craft.** In many cases, you don't even need to leave the house or office to do this. It's incredible how many instructional videos there are on YouTube or other online resources. In other cases, like with woodworking or ceramics, you'll need supplies.

- **Play chess or some other game.** This doesn't even need to involve another person. You can play against your computer. Maybe you can set a time to work on a crossword puzzle. There are all kinds of studies linking game playing and puzzles with cognitive benefits. They can certainly be relaxing and stress reducing activities.

- **Take up quilting, knitting, or crocheting.** I've personally never tried any of these, but my wife has. They seem like very relaxing activities, and when you're done, you've created something that you can cherish or give away as a gift. Also, it's been proven working with your hands is good for your mental health.

- **Take up painting or drawing.** I have done this, and it can be quite relaxing and gratifying. I've found that the paintings I've most enjoyed working on were those I was creating to give away as gifts to family and friends. As with other projects, I would often set a daily goal for making progress on a painting.

- **Watch birds.** This hobby seems to be more popular than ever. You don't need to travel to exotic places; you can find interesting birds in your yard or local park. We had the good fortune to have bald eagles and great horned owls within minutes of our home, and made time to go see them while the opportunity was there.

- **Read for pleasure.** Many of us spend time reading on the job. Reading at our leisure is an entirely different experience. No matter your interests, there are countless books out there that can teach you something and bring you joy. Maybe set a time and place for reading something enjoyable.

- **Explore your ancestry.** I've done this and it's fascinating. I created a family tree and learned what various nationalities and regions are part of my heritage. Through the service I use, I have access to a list of people and their relationship to me, based on DNA testing.

- **Watch the sunset.** It's a great way to bring the daytime to a close. But it's amazing how many times we forget to look toward the west when the sun is moving toward the horizon. Leave yourself a note or set your alarm. If you happen to live in a place where there is water to the west, you get an even more impressive view. Sunrises are nice too.

- **Enjoy the night sky.** It's amazing how much you can see in the sky at night, even if you live in a city with bright lights. I've spent countless hours looking through my telescope at the moon and planets, or watching meteor showers, or following the International Space Station, or just gazing at the stars. Some of the most transcendent moments I've experienced happened when I was enjoying the magnificence of what we can see of the universe.

I'm sure you can come up with plenty of other things to do that involve setting daily goals. And you don't need to take a drill-ser-geant approach to meeting your objectives. Just do the best you can to achieve what you want to do. Setting and achieving daily goals can be a tremendously rewarding experience. Why not make it a goal to do this?

19

PRACTICE HUMILITY

n 1984, I had the good fortune to be at the Summer Olympics in Los Angeles covering the technology in use at the Games for *Communications Week*, the publication I worked for at the time. In my free time, I went to some of the events, one of which was the boxing competition. It was the finals, and the arena was packed. During a break, I went to a concession stand to buy a snack, and as I waited in line I glanced over to my right. Standing just a few feet away was Muhammad Ali, a boxing legend and one of the most famous people in the world.

There was no entourage around him, and he was gazing up at the list of items for sale, just like the rest of us. The moment was memorable not because I was so close to a superstar, but because that superstar was doing the same thing I and countless other attendees were doing. It was a perfect picture of humility.

We live in a society that frequently places a high value on promoting ourselves and being assertive. It encourages competition, achievement, recognition, and status. Some people think humility is a sign of weakness, insecurity, or self-deprecation. It's not hard to see why this is an environment that can make it difficult to be humble. The truth is, we could all stand to be more humble. Humility involves thinking about others, being open to learning new things, and being willing to grow. It can strengthen our relationships with others and, ultimately, give us a more balanced perspective on life.

Unfortunately, humility, like patience, is one of the most difficult attributes to master. Many of us have a natural inclination toward thinking about ourselves and protecting our self-esteem and identity. We don't like to acknowledge our flaws or limitations. Oftentimes we don't feel like we need to learn new things because we already have the knowledge. Or we don't feel as if we need to improve our behavior or keep our relationships on an even keel. Our pride tells us we don't need help from others, that we can do it ourselves. Our ego makes us disregard constructive criticism.

I want to point out that I don't think there is anything wrong with having self-esteem and self-respect. Aiming for success in life is what we should be doing. And feeling satisfaction with ourselves after accomplishing something is a good thing. But when we tip the scales too far in the direction of pride and smugness, that's a different story. When we shut out others and refuse guidance from anyone, we're headed for disaster. And when we focus so much on ourselves at the cost of having empathy and concern for others, we've given up some of our humanity.

Humility is intertwined with equality, because humility involves acknowledging the inherent worth and dignity of everyone. It fosters a sense of shared humanity. We're all humans. We live on the same planet, breathe the same air, and are warmed by the same sun. We all need water, food, and shelter to survive. And we all have hopes and dreams and fears.

When you come right down to it, none of us is better than anyone else. We might have different talents, abilities, strengths, socioeconomic status, cultural influences, and opportunities. Instead of judging each other, we can celebrate our uniqueness and diversity. But at the most basic level, we are equal because we're all human beings. All humans are 99.9 percent identical in their genetic makeup, according to the National Human Genome Research Institute.

A lot of us are in awe of celebrities. Like my experience of waiting in line with Muhammad Ali, when you have an up-close encounter with someone who is famous, you get a thrill. It's sometimes difficult to relate to those people because they are famous. And it's sometimes easy to relate to them because they are human, just like us. I've read a lot of biographies and autobiographies, and it's always appealing when I learn about how well-known or heroic people can be humble. Abraham Lincoln is one of my personal heroes. I've been fortunate to visit the Lincoln Memorial in Washington, D.C. many times, and I never cease to be in awe of the monument and of the man it honors.

After being elected President of the United States, Lincoln went about creating his cabinet. Rather than choosing yes-men who would only follow his lead, he chose his fiercest political rivals, including men who had themselves sought to be President. This was a demonstration of Lincoln's humility and a willingness to learn from others. As described in Doris Kearns Goodwin's book *Team of Rivals*, this not only demonstrated Lincoln's political genius, but his ability to build a strong and united cabinet by including men with strong credentials who would help shape his policies.

Humility can be a good thing even when it's forced upon us. Following the cardiac arrest, I lost my driving privileges. It's not that I can't physically drive. It's that I'm taking medication that makes driving a risk. And given that I've had one cardiac arrest, if, heaven forbid, I should have another, I would not want to be behind the wheel of a car heading sixty miles per hour down a busy highway or on a neighborhood street.

Losing my left foot also presents some limitations. It makes me more prone to falls and prevents me from walking up or down really steep hills or on especially difficult terrains. Without my prosthetic, I'm reliant on a walker or wheelchair to get anywhere. I didn't want these things to happen, but they did and I've needed to adapt accordingly. It hasn't meant giving up and losing hope. It has involved recognizing and accepting my limitations and imperfections and adapting as needed or increasing my reliance on others for help. I'm fortunate to have a wife who does not object in the least to driving me wherever I need to go. If she is not available, there is always Uber or a neighbor, family member, or friend. I never feel like I'm stranded or inconvenienced.

I do now and then miss the independence of hopping in the car and driving somewhere. But I've grown accustomed to the idea that it's not something I should do. And I'm doing well enough with walking. Thanks to the prosthetic, I can walk fairly normally on smooth surfaces. I've learned what I can and cannot do, and that's working for me. Before I had the prosthetic, I did rely on those devices and the experience gave me a greater understanding of and empathy for the struggles people must face when they are unable to walk, even with a walker, cane, or crutches.

I have also experienced the opposite of humility. That is, ego and arrogance. The first of two kidney transplants I underwent took place at a prestigious hospital in Boston. The surgeon was known for his success rate with transplants. Prior to the surgery, I'd been experiencing blood clotting issues for several years that had complicated a few minor procedures. I thought it important to notify the transplant surgeon about the clotting problem as I was being prepped in the operating room. It was last-minute, but not too late. I asked him what precautions he was planning to take, and the surgeon assured me that the problems I'd experienced would not be a concern.

Sure enough, the transplant was not successful. There was no blood flow through the kidney and it wasn't functioning at all. The surgeon said he could go back in to try to fix the problem, and I gave my consent for him to do so. When I woke up from this procedure, Reneé was standing by my side, holding my hand. She told me they had to take the kidney out because it could not be revived. She had tears in her eyes but was smiling the same warm smile that has given me so much comfort so many times.

Apparently, the kidney had clotted off almost immediately after the transplant surgery. It had never worked at all. My thoughts immediately went back to the moments before the operation, when I had alerted the surgeon about the clotting problems I'd had. I felt my anger building, wondering why the surgeon had not done something to avoid this. It was pure arrogance on his part. He simply thought he was too good at what he did to listen to a patient.

By the time the surgeon stopped by my room, I had cooled off a bit. He looked devastated and on the verge of tears. He recalled my mentioning the issue, acknowledged his failure to take precautions, and apologized. I'd wanted to criticize him but I could see he was already miserable enough. The transplant coordinator at the hospital, who happened to be the surgeon's wife, told me later she had never seen him so distraught.

I'll never know if that kidney, so generously donated by a kindly soul, was destined to work. And to be clear, I want my doctors to be self-assured and confident. But not at the cost of being too prideful to listen to others even when something so consequential is on the line.

There is a religious and spiritual aspect of humility. As a Christian, I must acknowledge my need for God and believe that there is a divine plan that somehow encompasses all of us. Oftentimes this plan does not go the way we want it to go, but the acceptance of a divine plan can bring us peace. The Christian perspective on humility is similar to the secular view. We are not to think too highly of ourselves and instead prioritize the needs and wellbeing of others. And we're to acknowledge our limitations and dependence on God, rather than boasting about our abilities and achievements.

Of course, in this context, humility requires faith. The model is Jesus, who lived a life devoted to service to others, self-sacrifice, and obedience to God the Father. Humility and faith are intertwined. Humility enables us to trust in God's wisdom rather than our own understanding and experience. No matter how much we like to think we are in control of everything, we are not. Sure, we can control many aspects of our lives, such as how we behave in a given situation, where we live, what we do for a living. But when it comes to mapping out the grand plan of our lives, more things than we realize are out of our hands.

Because of pride, many of us have a hard time dealing with this lack of control and dependence on a divine being. I know I have. When things don't go the way I'd like them to, I often react with frustration. I've gradually learned that anger and resentment at my inability to control certain things can only lead to more stress. Again, I think of the first part of the "Serenity Prayer"—we need to accept the things we cannot change.

To wrap up, here are some ways I've learned about how to express humility:

- **Put others first.** This might seem counterintuitive when we're so inclined to seek our own happiness. But being there for others when they need you can be a source of joy.

- **Acknowledge your mistakes.** Also counterintuitive because no one likes to admit when they are wrong. Doing so shows that you can take responsibility for your actions, a sign of humility and strength, rather than weakness.

- **Seek advice and feedback.** We all need guidance from time to time. Recognizing that you don't know everything and being open to new ideas and different perspectives from others is also a sign of strength and humility.

- **Celebrate the successes of others.** When someone else succeeds at something or comes into good fortune, it's easy to be envious. But that leads to emotional pain. Being genuinely happy for others makes you a part of their success.

- **Share credit.** It's rare that anything we achieve is due solely to our own abilities. When we acknowledge the contributions of others and give them the credit they deserve, we reinforce the idea that we are dependent on others.

20

READ ALL ABOUT IT

There is something truly magical about a good book. It allows you to live in the moment because your focus is on the words, sentences, paragraphs, and pages that for a brief time grab your attention and perhaps transport you to a different place and time. Reading books is not just enjoyable. It can be thought-provoking, uplifting, educational, and inspiring as well. It can lift us out of the doldrums and provide us with just what we need in the midst of life's ups and downs. Reading can allow us to experience new things and visit new places. As Dr. Seuss (Theodor Seuss Geisel), noted in his book, *I Can Read with My Eyes Shut!*, "The more that you read, the more things you will know. The more that you learn, the more places you'll go."

For as long as I can remember I've enjoyed reading books. And I cherished the time I spent reading books to Andrew and Tim when they were young. Some of those books I would read over and over again at their request, and I never got tired of those stories. In recent years, my appreciation for them has grown with events like the Covid lockdowns that kept us mostly indoors, as well as some significant downtime because of health issues.

Here's a list of books I have found to be helpful in providing inspiration, comfort, guidance, entertainment, and joy. This is by no means an exhaustive list.

- *The Book of Joy: Lasting Happiness in a Changing World*, by the Dalai Lama and Archbishop Desmond Tutu. In this book, the two men look back on their long lives to answer the question of how we can find joy in the face of life's inevitable suffering and hardship. Over a week-long get-together, they trade intimate stories, tease each other, and share their spiritual practices. Because it's so personal, the messages come across clearly and effectively. One of these is how to confront the obstacles of joy, challenges that nearly all of us face now and then. My favorite part is the Eight Pillars of Joy, a list that includes perspective, humility, humor, acceptance, forgiveness, gratitude, compassion, and generosity.

- *The Boys in the Boat*, by Daniel James Brown. An inspirational story about the members of a University of Washington rowing team, and others associated with them, in their quest to win gold at the 1936 Olympics. It covers themes such as resilience and determination in the face of extreme adversity, and the power of teamwork and unity. It's about how a group of individuals, dealing with personal as well as societal challenges, came together to achieve a goal that seemed impossible. I'm drawn to underdog stories, and this was certainly a good example.

- *The Boy, the Mole, the Fox and the Horse*, by Charlie Mackesy. The characters—a curious boy, a greedy mole, a wary fox, and a wise horse—share a series of profound conversations about the meaning of life and other topics. It's a heartwarming story of unlikely friendships and self-discovery, accompanied by great artwork that lets you visualize the characters as they journey through a landscape reflecting their inner and outer worlds. It covers themes of compassion, loneliness, courage, hope, and connection with others. The characters learn to support and take care of each other, and they offer great lessons about life. I found myself relating to each of the characters at one point or another.

- *A Christmas Carol*, by Charles Dickens. There's a good reason why so many versions of this tale have been produced across various media including film, stage, and television. It's a great story and a timeless tale about transformation, empathy, compassion, generosity, and social responsibility. When I read this book, or watch one of the adaptations, I'm left wondering about where I fit on the spectrum of these virtues. How much have I felt empathy for others? How generous and kind have I been? How can I improve myself? This story is not only entertaining, but also continually enlightening.

- *Crossing the Threshold of Hope*, by Pope John Paul II. This book came out at a time when I was facing declining health from kidney disease. I was on dialysis and in need of a transplant, fearful and uncertain of the future, and this book provided some comfort and assurance. The title was appealing—we all need to have hope. It covers topics such as the existence of God, the dignity of man, pain and suffering, the relationship of Christianity to other faiths, and eternal life.

- *Don't Sweat the Small Stuff…and it's All Small Stuff*, by Richard Carlson. Many of us tend to blow things out of proportion, probably more often than we'd like to acknowledge. This book shows you how to avoid letting the little things in life get to you. It provides helpful advice about how to stay calm and put things in perspective in the midst of life's stressful situations. So many things can get on our nerves if we let them, and the chapters of this book provide ways to calm down. I found some of the most valuable lessons to be choosing your battles wisely, learning to live in the moment, and making peace with imperfection.

- *Have a Little Faith: A True Story*, by Mitch Albom. This book is about how the author goes on a spiritual journey to rediscover his faith. He witnesses the power of faith and the desire to help others in the midst of adversity, through his interactions with a Jewish rabbi and a Christian pastor. They each inspire him, and anyone who reads the book, to embrace hope and purpose in life. It's a story that might benefit anyone who has struggled with their faith and the meaning of life, as I have from time to time, with lessons about resilience, compassion, and having a positive outlook.

- *The Little Prince*, by Antoin de Saint-Exupéry. My memory is a bit fuzzy but I think I read this book in a high school English class, and to some degree it later helped inspire me to choose writing as a career. In any case, it inspires readers to reconnect with childlike wonder, playfulness, curiosity, and innocence. Other themes include finding meaning in simple things, the value of relationships, and looking beyond material possessions to seek what really matters.

- *The Lord of the Rings*, by J.R.R. Tolkien. This trilogy of books is a staggering achievement in writing. It's a sprawling epic fantasy that features an incredible amount of detail, complex characters, and a compelling narrative that holds your interest through three sizable books. In a short time, you begin to believe that Middle-earth is a real place, with its own geography (the books come with maps), history, and languages. Among the key themes are hope in the face of overwhelming odds, the importance of friendship, courage and selflessness, and perseverance despite adversity. I am in awe of Tolkien's ability to bring these fictional places and characters to life.

- *The New American Bible (Saint Joseph Edition)*. I have derived a lot of comfort and peace, as well as insights from reading the Bible. Some of the scriptures are easier to understand than others, and over the years I've read some books many times and others infrequently. But they all have valuable messages to apply to different situations in life. I like the description of the Bible in the introductory section, which calls it a "library of books, put together in one volume and authored over a period of many centuries."

- *Now is the Time: 170 Ways to Seize the Moment*, by Patrick Lindsay. A lot of our time is spent in idleness. We just want to hang out and do nothing, lacking the motivation to get started on something. I found this book easy to read and full of great suggestions of ways to embrace the moment and seize the day. Some examples: use your talents, confront your fears, look for hidden opportunities, ignore your limitations, care for our planet, and volunteer your time. If you're looking for ways to make better use of your time, this is the book for you.

- *The Official Honeymooners Treasury*, by Peter Crescenti and Bob Columbe. I feel like I have to include this book on my list because I'm a big fan of the classic television show, *The Honeymooners*. I can watch the episodes again and again and always enjoy some laughs. The book has a lot of detail about the show, including scripts, writers, plots, and actors. It also has trivia questions and answers, which adds to the enjoyment. Yes, you have to be a fan of the show to truly appreciate the book. I am, and I do.

- *Oh, the Places You'll Go*, by Dr. Seuss. As a father of two, I have enjoyed reading my share of great Dr. Seuss books. But none are quite like this one. Reneé got it for me as a birthday gift when I was going through a difficult time and feeling particularly disillusioned. It features all the charm, goofy characters, and great illustrations of a typical Dr. Seuss book. It also includes some great life messages, and encourages readers to find success from within, regardless of the challenges they face. We're all on a life journey that will have ups and downs. Despite the hardships, we all have the potential to achieve great things.

- *The Original Illustrated Sherlock Holmes*, by Arthur Conan Doyle. This is a big book that took me years to finish because I wanted to savor the stories, which include compelling characters and engrossing mysteries. It's fun to play detective as the tales unfold, not only to figure out who committed the crimes but how the master of observation and deduction would solve the mysteries. Each story comes with great illustrations, which adds to the effect.

- *Positive Thinking Every Day: An Inspiration for Each Day of the Year*, by Norman Vincent Peale. I try to read a page from this book every morning and have read the book multiple times over the years. It contains brief insights for each day of the year, and I've found many of these to be helpful. Not all of the messages resonate, and I sometimes forget them. But a lot of times, over the course of a year, just the right sentiment will jump off the page. What makes the book valuable is that its daily messages of inspiration and enthusiasm are timeless.

- *Seabiscuit: An American Legend*, by Laura Hillenbrand. This book about an underdog racehorse with incredible heart might seem like an odd choice to include. It offers some wonderful lessons about resilience, perseverance, overcoming adversity, the importance of teamwork, and others. It also happens to be one of my favorite books, written by one of my favorite authors. I bought it at a book sale at our sons' grade school, probably thinking it was more a matter of supporting a fundraiser for the school than acquiring a book I would actually read. I'm glad I bought it, and I'm glad I read it.

- *Team of Rivals: The Political Genius of Abraham Lincoln*, by Doris Kearns Goodwin. This is another one of my favorite books by another one of my favorite authors. It's a biography of Lincoln from a different perspective than I had heard of before. The focus is on how he assembled a cabinet of political rivals, men who themselves wanted to be President of the United States and had previously opposed Lincoln in the 1860 presidential election. The book examines Lincoln's ability to work with conflicting personalities and factions, and how this helped him lead the nation through the Civil War and the abolition of slavery. Reading this book only increased my admiration for the man.

- *A Year with Thomas Merton: Daily Meditations from His Journals*, by Thomas Merton. This is another book that is designed to be read daily over the course of a year. It includes inspirational and thought-provoking insights and observations drawn from the journals and papers of a Roman Catholic Trappist monk, writer, mystic, and peace and civil rights activist. I found that the book provides opportunities for self-reflection as well as spiritual guidance. It also features drawings and photographs by Merton.

A number of recent studies have shown that people, and children in particular, are reading fewer books than they used to. This saddens me because, apart from being a writer, I think many books truly have something to offer. We're never too young or too old to learn something new or to enjoy good stories.

There are also lots of studies that show how important it is for parents to read to their children, even when they are infants. My wife and I put great importance on reading to both of our sons on a regular basis when they were young. I have fond memories of reading books to them. I think I enjoyed the experience as much as they did. Some of the books we'd read over and over again, but they were always entertaining. I'm happy to say Andrew and Tim—who are both way smarter than me—continue to enjoy reading.

The widespread availability of eBooks makes it easier than ever to read books. If you don't feel like lugging a book around you can just take out your smartphone and read from it. The 95 Percent Group, which offers literacy tools and services for classrooms, in an article on its website entitled, "Why is reading important? The lifelong benefits of reading," cites these benefits to reading:

- Developing empathy
- Improving critical thinking skills
- Building vocabulary
- Enhancing conversation skills
- Learning social skills
- Strengthening cognitive processes
- Reducing stress
- Improving sleep
- Building and maintaining memory
- Strengthening writing, language, and communication skills

I hope I never get tired of reading. Whether it's books, magazine articles, essays, poems, short stories, or some other format, reading is a precious gift.

21

APPRECIATE THOSE WHO TEACH US LIFE'S LESSONS

S pend a few moments recalling some of the people who have influenced your life in some way. The more you think about it, the more you'll be amazed at how many have helped to make you the person you are today. We are fortunate to have an array of individuals who collectively inspire our identities—who we are, our values, beliefs, intellect, and behavior.

These are the people who, at different phases of life, play a role in building our character. They may come into our lives for a few moments or for decades, or play much bigger roles in our life journey. But all have some impact, and it's a good idea now and then to pause and pay tribute to the people who have influenced us.

OUR PARENTS

Perhaps no people shape who we are more than our parents. From the moment we are born they are teaching us life lessons. It's from our parents that we typically first learn about the importance of honesty, respect, fair play, responsibility, and good manners.

Our mothers and fathers teach us that we need to listen before we speak, to work hard in order to earn something, and to admit our mistakes and learn from them. They instruct us to look both ways before crossing a street. They explain patience, compassion for others, time management, and forgiveness. And of course, they teach us about gratefulness, to be thankful for what we have.

A lot of times, our parents teach us lessons not through words, but by how they conduct themselves. I saw both my parents work hard to support the family and make sure there was food on the table and a roof to live under. But they also took time for their four children, even when it meant sacrificing their spare time. When I played ice hockey as a teenager, we would frequently have games and practices at all kinds of odd hours. I don't remember either of my parents ever complaining about having to drive me to or from the rinks.

We also played games together, whether it was board games, ping-pong, or outdoor sports. I realize now that the hard work and the time spent together were expressions of love. One of my fondest memories from my younger years is playing Scrabble with my parents, just the three of us. I'd moved back home after my first job out of college vanished suddenly when the company went out of business. It was a difficult time emotionally for me because I was struggling with the career choice I'd made. But having my parents to myself for those moments, when I knew I had their unconditional love and support, meant the world to me.

OUR GRANDPARENTS

Grandparents can teach us many of the same lessons as our parents, but with the perspective and wisdom of having already raised children. They can also help to instill family traditions, provide their own unique perspectives on the past, and talk with us in ways parents can't or don't. Grandparents are able to tell us about life as it was many years in the past, which can be fascinating as they often have a wealth of life experiences to draw upon. And they can offer insights, advice, and wisdom by sharing anecdotes and passing down customs, providing us with a sense of heritage and identity.

Each of my grandmothers, whom we called Nonni, played a significant role in my life. We got to see a lot of my paternal grandmother, who lived nearby in New York City. During my visits to Greenwich Village, where she had an apartment, I was enthralled by how many people knew her as we walked around the neighborhood. This gave me a sense of the importance of community in our lives. In addition, her strong Catholic faith helped to strengthen my own.

My maternal grandmother lived in Montreal so I didn't get to see her as much, but whenever I did it was a memorable experience. She was as doting as you'd expect a grandmother to be and very demonstrative in her affection. Aside from her enthusiastic show of love, perhaps the biggest lesson I learned from her—as well as my father's mother—was independence. They each lived on their own, in city apartments, well into their golden years.

Unfortunately, I didn't really know my grandfathers. My mother's father passed away the week I was born and my father's when I was five years old. I wish I could have gotten to know them.

OUR SPOUSE/PARTNER

By the time you are done with school, out of the house, and old enough to get married, you would think you'd learned everything there is to learn. But that's not true, not by a long shot. Our spouses/partners can teach us many things, and this learning continues throughout married life. I think one of the most important things married couples learn is that marriage is a partnership, built on a strong foundation and grounded in faithfulness and trust.

Spouses can teach us about romantic love, how to be more compassionate and caring, commitment to a relationship, personal sacrifice, true friendship, putting someone else ahead of yourself, and being a good parent and child. When you're in a marriage for a long time, you have to be able to handle the ups and downs of life, the difficult times and the joyous times. Both partners should always be open to change and to adapting as needed by that change.

I know I've learned a lot from Reneé over nearly four decades of marriage. She has provided lessons in generosity, caring, responsibility, self-control, and gratitude—among others. Many times, these lessons were shown through her actions rather than words. For instance, her donating a kidney to me when mine were failing in the mid-1990s was the most selfless act I had ever seen anyone commit. On top of that, she disparages being called a "heroine," saying the decision to be a donor was something that seemed natural. This is one of many examples, and I'm grateful that Reneé has enabled me to continue learning life lessons, well into my sixties.

OUR CHILDREN

Sometimes, it's when we become parents ourselves that we first truly realize the enormous responsibility of being a parent. So perhaps one of the first lessons we learn from our children is how to be responsible for another person. They need us to survive, to learn, to grow. As our children grow up, they can remind us of how important it is to be curious about the world and to never stop asking questions and learning. All the "why" questions you get from your kids when they are little really do make you think about things that maybe hadn't occurred to you before, or not for a long time.

Children also teach us to use our imagination. Andrew and I spent hours in large cardboard boxes in the basement, pretending we were on a spaceship journey to some far-off location in the galaxy. And Tim and I built towns and zoos using wooden blocks and plastic animal figures. Being curious and using our imaginations can help us with solving problems and being more creative.

And children teach us to live in the moment. By engaging themselves fully in whatever project they are working on or fun activity they are involved in—completing a puzzle, splashing around in a pool, enjoying a playground—kids have a remarkable knack for living in the moment.

OTHER FAMILY MEMBERS

From our siblings we learn about sharing, fair competition, and trying to resolve conflicts. Our brothers and sisters are typically the first real peer group we have, and they help teach us how about loyalty and how to get along with others. It's not always easy growing up with others in the same household, competing for many things, including our parents' attention. One thing that's always there, though, is a bond that can bend but never break.

We can learn about the importance of family gatherings from our aunts, uncles, and cousins. Going to visit my relatives in Massachusetts and Montreal was always fun and gave me new perspectives about family ties and life in a different place than where I lived. I've mentioned the trip I took to Italy when I was young. It seemed like an entire village of family members made me feel at home in a foreign place, helping me to learn a new language and making a big deal out of having an American relative come to visit.

Our circle of family also includes our in-laws, and because Reneé also has a large family, I've been blessed with a lot of additional family members through our marriage. Over the years I've grown so close to some of them that there is essentially no distinction between blood and marriage relatives.

TEACHERS AND MENTORS

Teachers don't just instruct us on academic subjects like math, science, and English, they pass on lessons such as respect for others, perseverance, and the importance of setting goals and working hard. They teach us skills including how to learn from our mistakes, solve problems, and never stop learning. The best teachers I had, at least the ones I remember, were enthusiastic about their jobs. And I think that enthusiasm rubbed off on me and my fellow students. They got excited about what they taught, and that made it more intriguing.

One particular teacher from high school stands out. In grading a paper I wrote for English class, she said I should consider a career in journalism. No teacher had ever suggested a career for me before that. I took her advice, and it worked out pretty well from my perspective.

MEN AND WOMEN OF THE CLERGY

Clergy can teach us valuable lessons in faith, moral guidance, prayer, how to live a better life, and the importance of keeping God in our lives. Our faith might waver as we journey through life, but the basic lessons from clergy are always there.

Because I attended public grade school, I took classes in the Confraternity of Christian Doctrine (CCD), a religious education program in the Catholic Church that provides instruction to children who aren't enrolled in Catholic schools. The teachers, mostly nuns, helped prepare me for sacraments including First Communion and Confirmation. But they also taught me to try to be kind and respectful.

Throughout my adult life, I've been fortunate to receive spiritual counseling and support, particularly during difficult times.

OUR FRIENDS, NEIGHBORS, AND ACQUAINTANCES

Friends can teach us valuable life lessons about loyalty, compromise, communications, and, of course, friendship. We are social creatures, which is why friendships are so important. Along with family, they provide us with a vital support system. They accept us, even with all our flaws.

I've been blessed to have friends and neighbors who have offered support during difficult times. Two of my oldest friends, one who I've known since first grade and the other since college, have been sources of encouragement and strength. So have my neighbors. We've lived in the same house in Massapequa Park, N.Y. (named the best place to live in New York State by *U.S. News and World Report* in 2025!) for nearly forty years. We've had some wonderful neighbors who have shared many lessons about generosity and caring.

Then there are the people who pass briefly through our lives, but have a major impact. When I was working in my dad's store in the summers of the early 1970s, there was a Black gentleman who would come into the store once in a while. I would take a break from work and he and I would chat about any number of things for the brief time he was in the store. I grew up in an exclusively white neighborhood and hadn't known many African Americans. This man, who was one of the sweetest and most engaging people I've ever met, taught me the valuable lesson that the color of our skin does not—or should not—matter.

OUR COUNSELORS OR THERAPISTS

Counselors and therapists can teach us lessons in coping, communications, self-awareness, and how to deal with life's challenges. If they are good at what they do, they enable us to speak as honestly as possible about ourselves, our emotions, our behaviors, and our thought processes—something not a lot of others in our circle of life can do.

I've seen my fair share of psychotherapists in my time, largely to help me cope with a number of significant health issues. I'm not at all ashamed to admit this, even though there is a persistent stigma attached to needing emotional counseling. My philosophy is that taking advantage of this kind of help is not a show of weakness, but a demonstration of strength. Life is not easy, and we all need help now and then.

When I was on dialysis years ago, I told a psychologist during a session that I couldn't shake the self-image I had of being a sick person. I was defining myself as a patient and it was dominating my thoughts. The man thought about this briefly, and then told me to think of all the things I was other than a patient: a husband, father, son, sibling, uncle, friend, coworker. He suggested I constantly remind myself of all these associations. "When you're at the doctor's office, you're a patient," he said. "When you're anywhere else, you're a complete person who happens to have an illness that you're doing your best to treat."

OUR COWORKERS AND BOSSES

We can also learn valuable life lessons from the people we work with and work for, including interaction, responsibility, leadership, time management, and teamwork and collaboration. A typical workplace will have diverse personalities, which can help us learn about different perspectives and alternative ways of doing things. Though I began working at home many years ago—long before it was made popular by Covid—one of the things I've missed most about not working in an office with others is the camaraderie. I've worked with many dozens of people in various workplaces, and not always seen eye-to-eye with everyone. But many of these coworkers and bosses had positive things to share.

I've mentioned that one of my first jobs was with a company that had a work environment that was not especially pleasant. The owners could act like tyrants and the stress level was high. But the employees, the people who worked for them, were as nice as could be. We stuck together, and learned a lot from each other.

OUR PETS

Yes, we can learn a lot from our pets. Pets teach us lessons about unconditional love, patience, trust, loyalty, and responsibility. They seem to sense when we're not in a good place and give us extra attention.

We've had two dogs and eight cats over the years, each with a unique personality and appearance. They have been great sources of humor and entertainment. Some have been a bit more sociable than others, but all have been friends in their own way.

At no time is their appreciation for us more evident than when we come home from a vacation trip. As soon as they hear the front door open, they come to greet us, seemingly happy as can be (or, in the case of the cats, maybe briefly annoyed that we were away). Either way, they make us feel wanted and appreciated.

STRANGERS

When you think about it, the vast majority of people you encounter in life will be strangers, people we typically come into contact with only briefly. Or we might see them regularly but still don't know them, such as people on the train, subway, or bus on your morning commute, or the people walking along the sidewalk in a busy city. They might even be people you work with or with whom you share connections.

Regardless, we can learn lessons from strangers, including politeness and generosity. I once went to our well-known local hamburger place, All American, which at the time was only taking cash payments. It was crowded, as usual, with a lot of people waiting in line eager to place their orders at the takeout windows. When my turn came to order and pay, I took out my wallet and discovered I only had a few dollars. I was mortified. A man standing next to me in a different line, someone I didn't know, instantly took out some money and paid for the order.

OURSELVES

Finally, we can learn from ourselves. Through our life experiences—good and bad—we learn about what's important to us, what we like and don't like, how we can contribute to the world through our talents and skills, and how to be loving to those around us. We also learn about the importance and power of gratitude. And I am deeply grateful for all the people who have had an impact on my life.

THE RIPPLE EFFECT IS REAL

Think about this: a single action you take today can potentially affect dozens, or even hundreds, of other people. Your action could lead to another, which leads to another, which leads to another, and so on. This is called the ripple effect, so named for its resemblance to how ripples spread across the surface of water after something disturbs it, and it's a powerful way to spread positivity— or, sadly, negativity—in the world.

With the ripple effect, one event produces effects that spread and produce additional effects. This can apply to virtually every aspect of life, including families, larger social circles, economics, business, politics, religion, entertainment, and other areas. And it can apply to each of us as individuals. Yes, we can all create ripple effects without even realizing we are doing so. What an awesome, and frightening, thing!

The ripple effect works in both directions, for good or for bad, as life so often teaches us. One example of a negative ripple effect is a pandemic such as Covid-19, where it is likely that a few infected people inadvertently caused others to get the virus—in many cases without realizing it. From this, the virus rapidly spread and led to a historic, global calamity. It nearly brought the world to a standstill, and to date has resulted in more than 600 million known cases. It has altered the way we think about a lot of things, particularly how vulnerable we all are.

Another example of a negative ripple effect might be when a chief executive at a company makes a decision that leads to many layoffs at the business. This results in the laid-off workers changing their spending habits, which could then impact the very small companies that rely on their business. Some actions, such as declarations of war, economic sanctions, and other political activities can have massive ripple effects. On a more individual level, a negative ripple effect might be when a parent physically abuses a child, who then becomes a schoolyard bully who picks on another student, who ends up being psychologically scarred by the experience.

I want to focus on the positive aspects of the ripple effect, though. I think this description by the Devereux Center for Resilient Children, an organization that promotes the social and emotional development of children, summarizes the idea nicely: "One of the most beautiful aspects of kindness is its ability to create a ripple effect. When you're kind to someone, it often inspires them to be kind to others. This simple act of goodwill can set off a chain reaction of positivity that can touch countless lives. The smile you share with a stranger may brighten their day and encourage them to do the same for someone else. It's a powerful cycle that multiplies the impact of kindness exponentially."

Most of us come into contact with multiple people through the course of a day, whether it's face-to-face, on a phone call, via email or text messaging, or on social media. Each of these encounters or interactions offers an opportunity to begin a positive ripple effect. Here are few simple actions that could potentially result in a positive ripple effect. I've witnessed most of these, and I wonder what sort of impact these actions had beyond the immediate kindnesses:

- Paying someone at work or in your social circle a nice compliment

- Comforting someone who is having a difficult day

- Allowing someone to go in front of you in line at the grocery store

- Visiting a sick or homebound relative or friend

- Calling someone you haven't spoken with in a long time and talking about old times

- Acknowledging a coworker's efforts on an important project for the department

- Expressing your sincere gratitude for a kind gesture by your neighbor

- Donating time or money to a cause

- Providing a good piece of advice to a child or student

As I mentioned, these are simple things we can do without much effort. Your actions are not likely to result in major world occurrences, and they might not have an immediate impact. But even the simplest act of kindness can ultimately go a long way.

When I first began writing a blog about gratitude and positivity in June 2023, I wrestled with whether it was worth the effort. Then someone mentioned that I might never know the overall positive impact it could have through the ripple effect. It might start with a single reader who was moved by a particular post, who would then pass along the goodwill to someone else, and so on. That promise of a potential ripple effect and positive impact is what helps encourage me to keep at it. I understand that helping out even one reader is a good thing. So much the better if the impact is larger.

Sometimes we affect people in a positive way and don't even realize it for a long time. One day I was talking on the phone with someone I had worked with thirty-some years before. I had interviewed and recommended him for his job, and then became his manager after he was hired. As we caught each other up about what had been going on in our lives, he casually mentioned the impact I'd had on him as his mentor. This included his work ethic and professional values. I was touched by this, not having fully understood my impact on him. This individual has gone on to have a successful career, influencing countless people through articles, websites, and business conferences. I'd like to think that perhaps my influence on him has somehow had a positive effect on other people who then passed that positivity on to someone else, and so on.

We can influence so many people in our lives to set off a ripple effect. It can be our children, spouses, others in our families, friends, colleagues, teammates, teachers—even total strangers. Nearly everyone we come in contact with can be a potential source of a positive ripple effect.

On the other side of this coin, think of how many times you have had something done for you or said to you, and then that in turn led you to do something positive or influential. It really is mind-blowing to think how much impact we can have, not only on those around us but on people we might never know. In a May 2021 article in *Psychology Today*, Dr. Robert Puff, a clinical psychologist and host of the

Happiness Podcast, had this to note about the ripple effect: "We have a dangerous tendency to think that our actions only affect the people that we direct them to, but I believe the impact of our actions extends out further than we may ever know. Because of this, it's important that we begin being more thoughtful about our actions and words."

This is so true. There is a lot of negative energy in the world, manifested via wars and other conflicts, political factions, disparities of wealth, media coverage, fear, anger, and jealousy, envy, and so on. Anything we can do to add some goodness to our tiny part of the world is worth the effort, especially if it can have a broader impact than we can imagine. The ripple effect is not something that can be tangibly measured. There's no science behind it—and believe me, I checked. We can only do our part to spread goodwill, positivity, charity. If what we do ends up launching a positive ripple effect, so much the better.

Some time ago I took a Master Class in mindfulness by Jon Kabat-Zinn, professor emeritus of medicine and creator of the Stress Reduction Clinic and the Center for Mindfulness in Medicine, Health Care, and Society at the University of Massachusetts Medical School. Toward the end of the program, he offered these thoughts that I think sum up the idea of the ripple effect: "The world absolutely needs every single one of us to contribute in whatever ways we can, which we might think are far too small to be significant. But there's no such thing as insignificant. The people you touch in the world with your kindness, with your generosity, with your clarity, with your stability of mind, you may not know that you've ever had that effect on them. It may all happen wordlessly, but that's how the love spreads."

So the next time you perform an act of kindness, or a series of positive actions, take a moment to think about how much those gestures, over time, might help make this a slightly better world.

23

WE NEED EACH OTHER—
AND THAT'S A GOOD THING

Some time ago, I was visiting a local park with Reneé and a long-time friend from New York City, Howard Katz. It was a beautiful, early spring day, and we were enjoying the tranquil scene before us that included five ospreys soaring gracefully over a placid lake. Suddenly, a swan flew right over us and crashed loudly through a thick growth of reeds before landing clumsily in the water. For a few moments, the swan didn't move, and I was concerned that it was badly hurt.

After a few moments had passed, the swan recovered and began swimming slowly away from the shore. But the most startling thing about the episode was that within seconds of the botched landing, a large number of other swans from different areas of the lake began heading toward the fallen swan. There was no malice or aggression in their actions. They were just swimming gracefully but quickly toward their fallen comrade, appearing to be coming over to make sure it was okay. The three of us stood there watching, amazed at the sight. We had never seen anything like it.

Earlier that day in the same park, we had seen a great horned owl and her owlets perched in a tree. The mother owl was being quite attentive and protective, making sure that her babies had enough to eat and keeping a sharp lookout for any predators.

These unrelated nature activities set me to thinking about how much we all rely on others. Whether it's our spouse or partner, parents and other immediate family, extended family, friends, acquaintances, coworkers, associates, teachers, medical personnel, social groups, or others, we thrive—and even survive—because of them. Many of us like to think we are independent. I used to feel that way a lot and sometimes still do. But as I've learned from experiencing some major health issues, being independent is not always practical or possible.

That might not be a bad thing. A lot of times we need help from other people, and should count ourselves fortunate when others are available to provide that assistance. I know I wouldn't be around to write this book if not for the help of many people over the years. Even beyond the need for help because of a health problem or other crisis, having other people involved in our lives is important to our ability to function, live in harmony, and thrive. Plus, our need for each other can generate feelings of satisfaction and joy, whether we are the one in need or we are helping out someone else in need.

Years ago, several weeks after my kidney transplant from Reneé, there was an overnight winter storm that left a decent amount of snow on the ground. Neither one of us was in any condition to shovel, but we went to bed thinking we'd figure something out. The following morning, we looked outside to see that our sidewalk, driveway, and walkway to our house had been shoveled. We were extremely grateful for this act of kindness, not just because it got us out of shoveling, but because we knew someone was looking out for us. We strongly suspected our neighbors across the street for the good deed, although they never really admitted to being our snow angels.

A number of years later, those same neighbors were dealing with their own health issue. One winter day there was another big snowstorm, and we joined in with other neighbors to shovel their property. It felt great to be able to help people in need. It didn't matter so much that these were likely the same people who had helped us out years before. I didn't look at it as some kind of payback. It was more a matter of trying, in some small way, to help some fellow travelers in this journey of life in their time of need.

The American Journal of Lifestyle Medicine, in an October 2015 report, points out, "Humans are wired to connect, and this connection affects our health. From psychological theories to recent research, there is significant evidence that social support and feeling connected can help people maintain a healthy body mass index, control blood sugars, improve cancer survival, decrease cardiovascular mortality, decrease depressive symptoms, mitigate post-traumatic stress disorder symptoms, and improve overall mental health."

This perspective on relying on others, from a November 2021 article by professional healthcare consultant Jim Haggerty, "Relying on Others is Not a Bad Thing—In Fact It's Important," sums it up well: "When we can rely on other people, we are being genuine and recognize that we cannot do everything alone. This humbling feeling is important in developing as individuals and within a community. Many may fear asking for help, because of worries that it may make us feel insignificant. In reality, asking for help and allowing gratitude to flow through you can help you feel happier as well."

Those who help others through efforts such as volunteering can actually help themselves in the process. Scientific research over the years has shown that there are links between volunteering and enhanced physical and mental health. By giving generously of our time, we can gain a greater sense of optimism and purpose.

One of the best things about needing or helping other people is that it gives us a chance to feel and express our gratitude. Here's Haggerty again to bring this point home: "We are not operating alone in this world, we are surrounded by an incredible number of individuals who are just as complex as we are, and doing just what we are trying to do too—be human. Being grateful means feeling appreciation and recognizing the value of others' actions." By putting gratitude ahead of pride and our sense of independence, we can not only accept our need for others, but embrace it as well.

Sadly, the national boundaries mankind has created all over the globe over the centuries, and the more insidious boundaries created by ideological differences, can sometimes make it difficult to remember that we are all human beings. Regardless of our nationalities, ethnicities, races, religions, and other differences, we are all basically the same, living on the same planet that against all odds can support human life. We're a community of humans who need each other.

The late NASA Astronaut Bruce McCandless, who flew two Space Shuttle missions and performed the first untethered spacewalk, had a great perspective—in more ways than one. From low Earth orbit, he noted in a YouTube video, "Tell Me A Story: You Can't See Borders from Space," you can see continents, islands, geographical configurations, but you cannot see political boundaries. "We are all astronauts, we are all crew members on spaceship earth," he said.

In the 1980s, when I traveled to China on a business trip, I went with some apprehension mixed with excitement and curiosity. Although the country was open to tourists from the West by that time, visiting there was still a significant undertaking. It was very much a controlled environment. The communist government had restrictions on where you could go, and there was a heavy military presence at places like the airports.

After being there for a few days, I began to feel more relaxed, and when I had some free time, I decided to take a long walk from my hotel in the outskirts of Beijing and venture into the countryside. It was a fascinating walk through a place drastically different from any place I've ever been to before or since. The standard of living at that time was extremely low, with many people housed in structures that were no more than piles of bricks. Most of the roads were unpaved.

But what captivated me the most was the local people. As I walked along through farmland and a small village, I drew a lot of attention because they weren't accustomed to Westerners venturing into their neck of the woods. I didn't feel threatened. In fact, I felt welcome. Although I didn't speak any Chinese and practically none of the people I met along the way knew any English, we were able to communicate. If I wanted to take a picture of a group of people I would point to my camera and they would nod and smile.

Although we were different from each other in many ways, we found a way to connect with each other. This venture off the beaten path in the shadow of the capital city of China was one of the most memorable parts of the trip. I felt a shared sense of our common humanity, and I think if I had needed help, they would have given it.

In a May 2014 article on its website, the U.S. Centers for Disease Control and Prevention says staying connected to others creates feelings of belonging and being loved, cared for, and valued. Having social connections is important to our mental and physical health, it says, and being connected to others helps protect against serious illness and disease. "High-quality relationships can help people live longer, healthier lives," the CDC notes, and social connection can help reduce the risk of chronic disease and serious illness such as heart disease, stroke, dementia, depression, and anxiety.

"People are social creatures by nature," the article asserts. "Our relationships with family, friends, co-workers, and community members are important to our survival. Stable and supportive relationships give us the support we need to cope with stressful life challenges. People with healthy relationships are more likely to make healthy choices that lead to better mental and physical health." Communities that offer supportive connections are important. "They can help create trust and resilience among community members in public places, such as neighborhoods, schools, places of worship, workplaces, [and] parks and recreation centers," the CDC says.

Regardless of where or how we connect with others, the fact is we need each other. It's part of being human, and it's a wonderful thing.

DON'T LET FEAR HOLD YOU BACK

We all have fears, and we all get anxious now and then. It's part of being human. Even the "bravest" people among us experience distressing emotions aroused by impending danger, pain, evil, and other threats to their wellbeing, whether these threats are real or imagined. The good news is there are ways to manage fear and anxiety so that they don't take over your life.

Fear and anxiety can come from an array of sources: past traumatic experiences, potential harm, specific objects or situations, judgement by others, darkness, failure, loss of control, loneliness, death and dying, and the unknown. They can also stem from mental health conditions such as panic disorder, post-traumatic stress disorder, and phobias. No matter the cause, we need to try to keep fear from holding us back, from robbing us of joy. We can't let it dominate our lives, or keep us from realizing our true potential. Imagine someone who could be a great author, actor, ballerina, athlete, or recording artist, who never realizes that greatness because of a fear of rejection.

There's a difference between fear and anxiety. Fear is an emotional response to an immediate threat that is present or clearly defined. Once the threat goes away or is resolved, the fear subsides. Fear can help us react quickly to a threat and survive. It can happen anywhere and at any time. Fear isn't a problem unless it becomes an irrational fear or doesn't correspond to the actual threat.

Anxiety is a longer-lasting feeling of worry or trepidation about a future or uncertain threat. While fear provokes a "fight-or-flight" response, anxiety can be a more persistent sense of uneasiness, and it can linger even when there is no immediate danger. When feelings of dread about something going wrong in the present or future last for long periods of time, they can disrupt everyday life. We might lose sleep or struggle to concentrate.

Long-term anxiety and fear can be overwhelming, especially if you don't know why you are experiencing them or if they feel out of proportion to the situation, according to the Mental Health Foundation, a U.K. charity focused on preventing poor mental health and building and protecting good mental health. The foundation's website suggests some practical actions to help relieve anxiety and cope with fears:

UNDERSTAND WHAT YOU ARE FEELING AND WHY

One of the first steps toward overcoming fears and anxieties is recognizing that you are feeling anxious and figuring out the source of the anxiety. It's hard to overcome a fear that you don't really understand. Pay attention to what you are feeling and maybe write down notes in a journal or talk to someone about it.

When you pinpoint certain triggers for your feelings of dread, you can learn to better understand or avoid them. So much of what makes us feel uneasy might be easily conquered, if we just know what it is! If you have a better understanding of what's making you fearful, you might find out that it's nothing to be afraid of.

MANAGE YOUR ANXIETY IN THE MOMENT

I know from experience that it is really easy to let anxiety spiral out of control. Something will trigger these feelings and the next thing I know I'm making the proverbial mountains out of mole hills.

You can do much to control your thinking. If you notice that you're starting to feel anxious, you can stop these feelings from becoming overwhelming by managing them in the moment, the foundation says. One way to do this is to practice mindfulness, which can reduce anxiety by encouraging awareness of the present moment. Mindfulness can help us become more aware of what we are thinking and feeling, including anxious thoughts and feelings, and learn to not get caught up in them.

FACE YOUR FEAR IF YOU CAN

Sometimes things that make us a bit fearful—even things that are designed to be fun—turn out to be a lot easier to handle than we thought. There's a roller coaster ride in Disney World in Florida called Expedition Everest. On a vacation trip there, my son Tim wanted to go on it with me. As I looked at the ride from a distance, I saw a section where the coaster went backwards and then made a big drop down the "mountain."

By thrill ride standards it might be a little tame, but it looked intimidating to me. Nevertheless, I went on the ride and ended up having a great time. Trying something that you fear gives you a chance to see that, in many cases, there is nothing to be afraid of.

TALK TO A TRUSTED FAMILY MEMBER OR FRIEND

Feeling frightened or anxious about certain things is normal. Don't be afraid—no pun intended—to talk with someone about it. Just discussing how you're feeling can help reduce the anxiety and fear and encourage you to seek more support if needed, according to the foundation.

If you feel confident that someone will respond supportively—your spouse, parent, friend, coworker—consider opening up to them about your feelings. I think most people are happy to be of help, especially if they are important to you.

ENGAGE IN PHYSICAL ACTIVITY AND FIND WAYS TO RELAX

Getting exercise, even just a short walk, can help you put aside worries. The body and mind are connected, and by engaging in some sort of physical activity you can give yourself a break from mental woes. Also, find ways to relax, whatever that might be for you. Being in a state of fear and anxiety can keep you from being relaxed, which only makes things worse. Finding meaningful ways to loosen up can be an enjoyable way to reduce the physical and mental stress brought on by fear and anxiety.

I would add to this list by saying that faith and spirituality can play a significant role in helping us to deal with fear and anxiety. If you are a person of faith, praying, meditating, and attending religious services or meeting with faith-based groups can help you deal with stress brought on by fear and anxiety. On the eve of my kidney transplant in 1995, my emotions were all over the place. I was both excited and terrified at the same time. I wasn't so much worried about my impending surgery, although I certainly had a healthy dose of nervousness because it is a major operation.

My bigger concerns were for Reneé's wellbeing and that the transplant be a success. As the donor, she was also facing a major operation. What if the transplant failed for whatever reason? How would I live with myself knowing she had made this sacrifice for nothing? I was remembering the failed transplant from the previous year. And even though the circumstances were different, I couldn't be sure everything would go smoothly.

That evening, we attended a Catholic mass service in the hospital chapel, joined by many of our family members. The chapel was relatively small and modest, with several rows of pews and a simple altar. It was also beautiful, in a spiritual sense. As soon as we walked in, I felt at peace. The mass was celebrated by a Franciscan brother who had come from Pennsylvania to fill in for the regular Catholic chaplain at the hospital. He spoke in a soft, soothing voice, and selected readings including this from the Letter of James in the New Testament:

> Is anyone among you suffering? He should pray. Is anyone in good spirits? He should sing praise. Is anyone among you sick? He should summon the presbyters of the church, and they should pray over him and anoint him with oil in the name of the Lord, and the prayer of faith will save the sick person, and the Lord will raise him up. If he has committed any sins, he will be forgiven.

The brother then gave a brief, but moving sermon. He talked about the importance of our families being there with us and their show of love and support at our time of need. It was a wonderful celebration and, as the service went on, I could genuinely feel the presence of God in the room. It was a positively glowing feeling unlike anything I had experienced. I also could feel the presence of Reneé's late mother and my grandmother who'd passed away years earlier. The warm, comforting feeling continued as the brother administered the anointing of the sick sacrament to both Reneé and I. This is typically given to people who are seriously ill or facing a physical challenge such as a major operation.

It was very quiet in the room as he conducted the rite. I held Reneé's hand tightly in mine. I could feel myself starting to get tears in my eyes as he continued his prayers and everyone responded with their prayers asking that we have successful operations. As in every Roman Catholic mass, there was an "exchange of peace" where you're supposed to greet the people around you, wishing them peace. When it was time for this, everyone in the room exchanged hugs, kisses, and wishes of peace. Reneé and I have talked about this many times since, that we could feel the enormous support from everyone there.

By the time the service ended, I felt as if something had changed. My nerves were calmer; I felt utter confidence that everything would go well the next day. Reneé and I were facing these operations, and I was facing the challenges of a kidney transplant. I was at peace with this. Afterward, when we gathered in the hospital cafeteria for sodas and coffee, it felt like a party. We joked and laughed. It seemed like everyone had drawn strength from the service. I know I did.

The phrase "fear not" appears many times in the Bible, and I think we need to draw comfort from that.

THE GREATEST OF THESE IS LOVE

S o faith, hope, love remain, these three; but the greatest of these is love" (1 Corinthians 13).

What would the world be like without love? What would your life be like? It's too difficult to ponder because it's unimaginable. Love is at the center of who we are as human beings. It's the complex emotion that outweighs all others in importance.

According to multiple research reports, love is valuable because it enriches our lives, fosters strong connections with others, improves our mental and physical health, enhances our self-esteem, promotes healing, and provides a sense of belonging, purpose, and support. Love leads to greater happiness and overall wellbeing. It helps us cope with stress, manage pain, and perhaps even live longer. And it can lead to other benefits such as improved communications, stronger social bonds greater empathy and compassion. In short, love is a basic human need that plays a vital role in our physical, mental, and social wellbeing. It gives us the support, connection, and meaning we need to thrive.

There are different types of love, including romantic and enduring love between spouses; familial love of parents, children, siblings, and extended family members; love of close friends; love of yourself; and universal, selfless love. This last one is called *agape* love, a Greek term that means charity or unconditional love. It is often considered the highest form of love.

I've been fortunate to experience all these types of love in my life, but I'd like to relay a love story that encompasses all of them. As I've mentioned in earlier chapters, I was heading into kidney failure in 1989 because of a condition called polycystic kidney disease (PKD), a chronic ailment that reduces kidney function over time. PKD is one of the most common genetic disorders, affecting some 500,000 people in the United States, according to the U.S. National Library of Medicine.

I'd been diagnosed at the age of nineteen, following an episode of high blood pressure that got my family doctor concerned. By the time I was in my early thirties, my kidneys had deteriorated to the point that I needed to start dialysis treatments. Having to survive by virtue of an "artificial kidney" was not an easy experience. There were dietary restrictions, risks including infection, and the psychological stress of being regularly reminded that I was chronically ill. However, the treatments enabled me to function as normally as possible under the circumstances.

Unfortunately, over time, the treatments became less and less effective. My doctors advised me to get on a waiting list for a transplant. I had mixed emotions about this. While it was clear I needed a transplant, I also knew this would be a major operation. In addition, I wasn't sure how I would feel about living with someone else's kidney.

In April 1994, I got a call alerting me that a kidney was available, so I headed up to a hospital in Boston where the transplant would take place. But as I've described already, the transplant did not work because of a clotting issue. This was a traumatic experience, but one of the positive takeaways was the knowledge that someone, a person whom I'd never met and never will in this life, was generous enough to be an organ donor. It was an act of selfless love.

Over the following months, my health continued to deteriorate as my kidneys failed. In the summer of 1995, when it became clear that I needed to get a transplant sooner than later, Reneé decided she would be tested to determine whether she would be a suitable donor. While I was extremely grateful for her incredibly generous offer, I declined. There was no way I was going to put Reneé at risk for something that might not even work. It would be better to take my chances and wait for another donor from the waiting list, I thought.

Knowing that time was of the essence, Reneé was determined to be tested, however long the odds that we would even be a good enough tissue type match for a successful transplant. One factor that contributed to her wanting to donate was an article she had read in the *New England Journal of Medicine* about the success of kidney transplants between spouses. And for what it's worth, the article was published on August 10th, which happens to be Reneé's birthday.

When the test results came back, we were astonished to learn that we were as good a tissue type match as if we were siblings. We took this as a sign that this was meant to be, and Reneé became even more enthusiastic about donating a kidney to me. This time around, I signed up for the transplant program at Westchester County Medical Center. When the transplant coordinator informed us of the next available date for the transplant, we were astounded. It was October 25th, our wedding anniversary.

For me, this sealed the deal. Despite my ongoing concerns about Reneé being a donor, I was convinced that this was the way things were supposed to happen. This was now not only selfless and unconditional love, but romantic love as well. A psychologist I was seeing at the time summed up the developments well: "This is a wonderful, terrific story. Especially for your son. He's going to be learning an invaluable lesson in character and love from the two most important people in his life."

Sensing a good news story and wanting to promote the cause of organ donation, I notified our local newspaper, *Newsday*, about the upcoming transplant. The editors agreed to do a story about us, and put it on the front page. This opened the floodgates, as dozens of other news organizations wanted to cover our story. Once we arrived at the hospital for the transplant, security personnel had to keep reporters from getting to our rooms. The publicity was extremely positive, with articles and television reports describing the wonder of a wife-to-husband organ transplant—on our anniversary, no less.

Adding to the positive vibe was the fact that many relatives from both sides of our family traveled to Westchester to support us. Most important, they supported our eight-year-old son Andrew, who had to go through the experience of having both parents undergo major surgeries at the same time. This is familial love. As I mentioned in the previous chapter, on the evening before the transplant we all went to the hospital chapel for a service. The feeling of love from the people closest to us was overwhelming.

We heard from friends who were kept informed of the ongoing events by family members, their support representing yet another kind of love. And in the bustle of all the pre-surgical events we had to remember the importance of self-love, appreciating ourselves and acknowledging our strengths and weaknesses as we approached this momentous event.

On the morning of the transplant, a nurse rolled my stretcher next to Reneé's in the operating room waiting area. We held hands and spoke to each other quietly while we waited for someone to come and get us. There was a sense of excitement and anticipation unlike anything we'd experienced before. It seemed like everyone there knew who we were and why we were there.

"It's amazing, I don't feel nervous about this at all," Reneé said. "I'm so anxious for you to get better. I keep thinking that this will be such a minor thing to go through for the chance to see you healthy again." Then, suddenly, the attendants were there for us. I leaned over to give Reneé a kiss. "I love you so much," I said. "Good luck, and I'll see you soon." She smiled and said, "I love you too, sweetheart," then we were on our way to separate operating rooms.

The transplant was a success, and nearly three decades later I'm happy and grateful to report that my kidney is working well. What a blessing. I'm forever grateful to Reneé for her selflessness and boundless love in stepping forward to be my donor. She is at the center of this tremendous love story.

Shortly after the transplant, I remarked to the surgeon that because the transplant had been such a success he was a hero to me and my family. "No," he said with a smile and shaking his head, "your wife is the hero." He was right, of course. It takes a special kind of person to make the kind of sacrifice Reneé made. Over the many years that have followed the transplant, she has never once said or done anything to make me feel as if I owe her anything. Whenever I mention to someone what a generous act this was, she says that what she did was out of pure love.

I've been very lucky to be in a loving marriage, and have a lot of people in my life who have been generous with their love. One of the silver linings of having challenges such as health problems is that it gives the people around you opportunities to show their love. I've seen this again and again, and it has cheered and comforted me in my times of need.

I've been fortunate to have a wonderful wife and sons, as well as extended family members, with whom to enjoy and appreciate the experiences of life and love. Much of this has been agape love, the selfless, unconditional acts that are the purest expressions of caring for others. We could all stand to practice more of this kind of love. Think of how much better the world would be if we did.

This love is driven by a desire for the wellbeing of others, putting their needs before our own. We choose to express this love without expectation of anything in return and without any sense of obligation. Think deeply of all the people in your life who have loved you in this way. You will be overwhelmed with gratitude and joy! And in return, there are countless ways you can express this kind of love for others. Here are just a few:

- Volunteer at a food bank or soup kitchen
- Visit someone in the hospital
- Visit someone in prison
- Help out at an animal shelter
- Volunteer for a literacy program
- Help out at a food drive
- Donate to a reputable charity

- Comfort a coworker or neighbor who is struggling

- Help out at a homeless shelter

- Donate blood

- Forgive someone who has wronged you

- Drive an elderly acquaintance to appointments

- Tutor students at local schools

We can find all kinds of ways to draw from our time, talent, and treasure to help our fellow travelers in this journey of life—all expressions of love—and in so doing, make the world a better place.

REFERENCES

A list of sources referenced in this book.

CHAPTER 1

"The Science of Gratitude," by Summer Allen, Ph.D., Greater Good Science Center at the University of California, Berkely, May 2018, https://ggsc.berkeley.edu/images/uploads/GGSC-JTF_White_Paper-Gratitude-FINAL.pdf

"Can expressing gratitude improve your mental, physical health?," by Amanda Logan, for Mayo Clinic Health System, Dec. 6, 2022, https://www.mayoclinichealthsystem.org/hometown-health/speaking-of-health/can-expressing-gratitude-improve-health

CHAPTER 2

"Toxic Positivity," *Psychology Today* (undated), https://www.psychologytoday.com/us/basics/toxic-positivity

"What Is Negativity Bias and How Can It Be Overcome?" by Catherine Moore, for PositivePsychology.com, Dec. 30, 2019 https://positivepsychology.com/3-steps-negativity-bias/#:~:text=Negativity%20bias%20is%20caused%20by,a%20form%20of%20self%2Dprotection

"Positive thinking: Stop negative self-talk to reduce stress," by Mayo Clinic staff (undated) https://www.mayoclinic.org/healthy-lifestyle/stress-management/in-depth/positive-thinking/art-20043950

"Four Simple Ways to Develop a More Positive Attitude," by Tchiki Davis, *Psychology Today*, Sept. 23, 2029, https://www.psychologytoday.com/us/blog/click-here-happiness/201909/four-simple-ways-develop-more-positive-attitude

CHAPTER 3

"Associations Between Procrastination and Subsequent Health Outcomes Among University Students in Sweden," Jan. 4, 2023 https://pmc.ncbi.nlm.nih.gov/articles /PMC9857662/

"Overcoming Procrastination," Johns Hopkins University Academic Support website, https://academicsupport.jhu.edu/resources/study-aids/overcoming -procrastination/

CHAPTER 4

"Regular crosswords and number puzzles linked to sharper brain in later life," University of Exeter and King's College London, *International Journal of Geriatric Psychiatry*, May 15, 2019, https://news-archive.exeter.ac.uk/2019/may/ title_716265_en.html

"Cognitive Distortions: Unhelpful Thinking Habits," by Dr. Matthew Whalley, Psychology Tools, March 18, 2019, https://www.psychologytools.com/articles/ unhelpful-thinking-styles-cognitive-distortions-in-cbt

"Ten Types of Cognitive Distortions," Dr. David D. Burns, Jan. 6, 2013, https://martinsetiabudhi.wordpress.com/2013/01/06/ten-types-of-cognitive-distortions/

CHAPTER 5

"Psychological Benefits of Routines," by WebMD editorial contributors, Sept. 20, 2024 https://www.webmd.com/mental-health/psychological-benefits-of-routine

CHAPTER 6

"Tips for embracing joy in daily life," Mayo Clinic Health Systems, March 23, 2023, https://www.mayoclinichealthsystem.org/hometown-health/ speaking-of-health/tips-for-embracing-joy-in-daily-life

The Book of Joy: Lasting Happiness in a Changing World, by the Dalai Lama and Archbishop Desmond Tutu, Avery, 2016

"Stress relief from laughter? It's no joke," by Mayo Clinic staff, Sept. 22, 2023

"Why Giving Is Good for Your Health," Cleveland Clinic, Dec. 7, 2022, https:// health.clevelandclinic.org/why-giving-is-good-for-your-health

CHAPTER 7

"It's Surprisingly Hard to Go to the Sun," by Sarah Frazier, NASA. Aug. 8, 2018

CHAPTER 8

"Starting bystander CPR within 10 minutes of cardiac arrest may improve survival," American Heart Association News, Nov. 11, 2024

"Positive Mindset: How to Develop a Positive Mental Attitude," by Courtney E. Ackerman, for PositivePsychology, July 5, 2018, https://positivepsychology.com/positive-mindset/#:~:text=It%20is%20looking%20adversity%20in,always%20 (Jarrow%2C%202012).

CHAPTER 11

"8 Health Benefits of Getting Back to Nature and Spending Time Outside," by Emily Swaim, for Healthline, May 28, 2022, https://www.healthline.com/health/health-benefits-of-being-outdoors#better-breathing

CHAPTER 12

"50 Tips for Practicing Mindfulness," by RocheMartin, Feb. 13, 2020 https://www.rochemartin.com/blog/50-tips-for-practising-mindfulness

CHAPTER 16

"How To Be Patient: 6 Strategies to Help You Keep Your Cool," Cleveland Clinic, June 5, 2024, https://health.clevelandclinic.org/how-to-be-patient

CHAPTER 19

"Genetics vs. Genomics Fact Sheet," by the National Human Genome Research Institute (undated), https://www.genome.gov/about-genomics/fact-sheets/Genetics-vs-Genomics

CHAPTER 20

"Why is reading important? The lifelong benefits of reading," the 95 Percent Group, https://www.95percentgroup.com/insights/reading-importance/?srslti d=AfmBOoqGauDH6h1G-Bo-F4wRStChkjapfsm47OA1Ot3_xSk_shj7IQes

CHAPTER 22

"The Power of Kindness: A Ripple Effect of Good," by the Devereux Center for Resilient Children, Nov. 6, 2023, https://centerforresilientchildren. org/powerofkindness/#:~:text=The%20Ripple%20Effect&text=When%20 you're%20kind%20to,the%20same%20for%20someone%20else

"Why Kindness Has a Ripple Effect" by Dr. Robert Puff, *Psychology Today*, May 28, 2021, https://www.psychologytoday.com/us/blog/meditation-for -modern-life/202105/why-kindness-has-a-ripple-effect

CHAPTER 23

"The Connection Prescription: Using the Power of Social Interactions and the Deep Desire for Connectedness to Empower Health and Wellness," *The American Journal of Lifestyle Medicine,* Oct. 7, 2015, https://pmc.ncbi.nlm.nih.gov/ articles/PMC6125010/

"Relying on Others Is Not a Bad Thing—In Fact, It's Important," by Jim Haggerty, Nov. 5, 2021, https://jameshaggertyrecovery.com/blog/relying-on -others-important/

"Social Connection," by U.S. Centers for Disease Control and Prevention, May 15, 2024, https://www.cdc.gov/social-connectedness/about/index. html#:~:text=Staying%20connected%20to%20others%20creates,against%20 serious%20illness%20and%20disease.

CHAPTER 24

"How to manage fear and anxiety," Mental Health Foundation, https://www. mentalhealth.org.uk/explore-mental-health/publications/how-overcome- anxiety-and-fear#:~:text=Manage%20your%20anxiety%20in%20the%20 moment&text=Try%20to%20find%20a%20comfortable,your%20body%20 change%20in%20response.

ACKNOWLEDGMENTS

First, a few words of thanks to those who helped in the creation of this book. My editor, Staci Frenes, provided insightful feedback on the manuscript as well as meticulous copy editing of the content. I appreciate her valuable guidance in helping to bring all the elements of the book together.

Thanks also to Michael Tizzano for proofreading the manuscript, Steve Kuhn for creating the cover and designing the interior of the book, and Heather Wallace for marketing guidance.

This book would not have been possible without the many people who have influenced my life in ways large and small. They are the ones who helped me to learn the important lessons life has to offer.

My sincere thanks to all who have provided me with inspiration, guidance, and moral support over the years. There are far too many individuals to mention, but I am filled with gratitude for everyone who has helped me navigate the challenges and embrace the joys of life.

This community of fellow travelers on my life's journey includes family members, friends, neighbors, teachers, coworkers, business clients and associates, mentors, clergymen, healthcare professionals, therapists, strangers, and countless others with whom I have interacted in some way.

A special thank you to my parents Joe and Edda Violino for being my first providers of life lessons, to my son Andrew and his wife Nikki and my son Tim and his girlfriend Victoria for giving me joy, hope, and support.

I can't thank my wife Reneé enough for being my constant source of inspiration and support, not only as I was working on this book but throughout our married life. She provided valuable input on the manuscript and other elements of the book. Even more important, she has been my soulmate for nearly forty years.

ABOUT THE AUTHOR

Bob Violino has covered some the most momentous events in the information technology field, including the emergence of the personal computer, the growth of mobile communications, and the rise of artificial intelligence, over a career spanning more than forty years. Since 2002, he has worked as a freelance writer, producing articles, newsletters, and other content for print and online publications and clients in a variety of industries. In addition to his personal blog, *Embracing Gratitude and Positivity*, Violino has authored the books, *New Life: Lessons in Faith and Courage from Transplant Recipients* and *Children of the Light.* He lives in Massapequa Park, New York, with his wife Reneé, and enjoys reading, blogging, travel, painting, and experiencing the wonders of nature.